An Inside Seat

An Inside Seat

A MEMOIR:
TRUE STORIES TOLD BY
SOUTH FLORIDA PR ICON
MAXINE ADLER

Maxine Adler
with Judy Goldstein

Foreword by Michele Kleier
Co-star of HGTV's *Selling New York*, 2010–14

Requests for permission to make copies of any part of the work should be submitted via e-mail to the authors at: aninsideseat@gmail.com.

Printed in the United States of America
ISBN-10: 1541266277
ISBN-13: 9781541266278
Library of Congress Control Number: 2016921348
CreateSpace Independent Publishing Platform
North Charleston, South Carolina
The recollections and stories shared are accurate to the best of the authors' knowledge. Although every precaution has been taken to verify the accuracy of the information contained herein, the authors assume no responsibility for any errors or omissions. No liability is assumed by the authors for damages that may result from the use of any information contained within. The authors are not liable if the reader relied on the material and was financially damaged in some way.

Dedication

To my beloved Owen—my husband, my lover, my partner, and my best friend.

"There is only one thing in the world worse than being talked about, and that is not being talked about."
Oscar Wilde
The Picture of Dorian Gray, 1891

Contents

Foreword · xi
Introduction · xiii

Chapter 1   When the Dust Settled · 1
Chapter 2   The Beginning · 3
Chapter 3   Planting South Florida Roots · · · · · · · · · · · · · · · · ·11
Chapter 4   The Silver Fox ·19
Chapter 5   For What It's Worth · 26
Chapter 6   On the Waterfront ·31
Chapter 7   Ar+Vi+Da ·47
Chapter 8   Sophia ·56
Chapter 9   My-T-Fine ·62
Chapter 10   The Great Gatsby ·70
Chapter 11   To the White House ·75
Chapter 12   East Meets West · 80
Chapter 13   The Donald ·89
Chapter 14   Miami Design District ·95
Chapter 15   An International Design Destination · · · · · · · · · · · 99
Chapter 16   Stitched at the Hip ·107
Chapter 17   A Forte for Fashion · 114
Chapter 18   Doing Things Differently · · · · · · · · · · · · · · · · · · ·126
Chapter 19   Confrontation amid the Palms · · · · · · · · · · · · · · · ·133
Chapter 20   The Quiet Trump ·136

Chapter 21	Imploded	144
Chapter 22	There's Never Been a Better Time to Buy	147
Chapter 23	Taking Its Toll	152
Chapter 24	Events R Us	155
Chapter 25	I'm Not Dead Yet	167
Chapter 26	Reality TV	169
Chapter 27	Venus, If You Will	175
Chapter 28	At the Movies	180
Chapter 29	Shorts	182
Chapter 30	Introspection	196

Afterword	199
Photography	201
Photo Credits	215
Acknowledgments	217
Word Play for PR Writer Wannabes	221
About the Authors	225
How to Order This Book	227

Foreword

By Michele Kleier

MAXINE ADLER IS A FORCE of nature. She cold-called me in 2010 to let me know she was representing the developer of a new oceanfront project located on the grounds of the Boca Raton Resort and Club's Boca Beach Club. She knew who my daughters and I were because of our visibility as co-stars on HGTV's hit reality series *Selling New York*, and she wanted us to help market and sell the luxury development. Although I told her ten different times, in ten different ways, that we didn't have Florida licenses, and we were only down there three times a year at most, we found ourselves shortly thereafter in our beach cover-ups, with kids in hand, touring the One Thousand Ocean construction site. This occurred over our Thanksgiving trip to Boca.

The spectacular fifty-three-unit seven-story building was under construction. And Maxine was sure we could help sell the building by featuring it on our TV show. It turned out that One Thousand Ocean's developer, LXR Luxury Resorts, also owned the Boca Raton Resort and Club, its Boca Beach Club, and the Waldorf Astoria in Manhattan, to name some of its renowned properties. Maxine literally held us captive there until Jamie Telchin, LXR's president of development, arrived to meet with us. The rest is history!

Our family had vacationed at the Boca Raton Resort and Club since our children were in nursery school. In fact, we always liked to sit at the very end of the beach, on the very site of One Thousand Ocean. So the girls and I felt an immediate emotional connection to the building and to Maxine, who like us, had a family business.

From the time I met Maxine, I related to her. Maybe it was because we both owned businesses and were deeply committed to our clients. She also told me that she and her husband, Owen, had been members of the Boca Raton Resort's Premier Club for many years; consequently, they frequently sat by the jetty at the Boca Raton Inlet to clear their heads. We had been in the exact same spot!

An Inside Seat is an informative and fun read for anyone in the public relations, marketing, real estate development, real estate sales, and design fields. It also will be of interest to anybody in any business, for that matter. In this book, Maxine takes you with her into the world she lived and loved for over forty years. We feel blessed to have met her.

Michele Kleier is co-president, Kleier Residential (formerly Gumley Haft Kleier), New York City. She was a co-star of HGTV's Selling New York, *2010–14.*

Introduction

NOW THAT I'VE ENTERED THE final turn in this journey that I call *life*, I am more comfortable in my skin than I have ever been. During these golden years, I embrace and celebrate them because I have lived a truly remarkable existence. For me, this is a time to reflect on my blessings and experiences and their outcomes. They are rich and full.

Like most seniors my age, some abilities have begun to challenge me. But my memory has not. It remains sharp as a tack. That's the reason why, at long last, I have written a book about some of my wonderful, and oftentimes unusual, career tales. I had always wanted to, and many of my colleagues urged me to do so over the years. They thought I had a lot to convey that could help others, while telling some of my favorite (and often funny) stories. But I never had the time.

In the September of my years, there's been much more time to look back than ahead. Even as I ease into retirement, my keen recollections keep the fire in my belly ablaze. I have no regrets about how hard I worked or the long hours I devoted to my clients. As the daughter of a retailer, I understood that customers need to be satisfied and, better yet, they should have their expectations exceeded. That was the mission that drove me, in addition to my own personal reward of self-satisfaction for a job well done.

Business stimulated me. I preferred sitting in a conference room rather than in a card room. As the owner of a minority-owned business, I never let being a woman stand in my way. That burning passion within my gut made me positive, tenacious, and tireless. I always saw the glass as half-full. Long meetings, endless deadlines, and the pressure to perform exhilarated me. I was a problem solver who enjoyed challenges. I was accessible to my clients and the press at all hours, day or night. I oftentimes played the role of a psychologist, even though I had no formal training. There were times when my clients confided things to me that even their attorneys or accountants didn't know. They trusted me as an insider and knew I would never reveal anything about them, or what they were doing, to their competitors. In addition, the media trusted the information I gave them. They knew that my sources were credible.

I began my career long before there was access to computers, twenty-four-hour cable news, cell phones, digital photography, e-mail, online press release distribution, and social media. I bought my first fax machine only because Tom Glass of the Roscioli Yachting Center, a client, had just purchased one, and he wanted to have someone to communicate with in this new and efficient way. Call me a dinosaur. I won't blame you. But I truly believe that life was far more personal and less complicated back then. Typing on a manual Royal or Underwood that had only one font and one type size, proofreading text on "flats," and viewing color transparencies with a loop on a light box weren't so bad. Then advanced technology reared its innovative head and the world exploded, becoming smaller as we became instantaneously connected with the click of a mouse. Public relations practitioners like me benefited by being able to reach out globally on behalf of our clients. This is something that today's young PR professionals are apt to take for granted.

My choice was to own and operate a small boutique public relations agency in South Florida. The Adler Network Inc. provided highly personalized service far beyond any nine-to-five work week. Along with my account supervisors, who were top-notch writers and event planners, we served our clients anytime, anywhere. We did it all. And *I* didn't disappear after the contract had been signed, turning over client responsibility to a novice.

People in the real estate development or real estate sales industries, as well as architects and interior designers, may enjoy my stories and derive ideas from them. And who knows? Maybe you'll even find your own name or project mentioned here.

My agency had the good fortune of having a true professional as part of its team—and my family—for eighteen of those years. That's as long as some marriages last! Because I believe that everything happens for a reason, it was surely fate that brought Judy Goldstein into my office in 1996. She played a colossal role in the Adler Network's success as it moved forward. To this day, Judy and I continue to feel a remarkable connection—a sisterhood, so to speak. This book was a collaborative effort that could not have come to life without her and her many talents.

If you are involved in the public relations industry, then you are likely to have had some experiences similar to mine. Like me, you too had an inside seat next to your clients and knew early on about things other people didn't, oftentimes before they happened. Such occurrences were not exclusive to my agency—except perhaps receiving a personal invitation to the White House or going toilet-seat shopping with a celebrity couple in Los Angeles! Add in other high-profile personalities, politicians, industry moguls, and a few convicted felons, and I have a melting pot of tales to tell.

Those of you who may be contemplating a public relations curriculum in college, or who already are a student, may get an entirely new perspective into the PR field after reading this book. I hope you will learn from it and that my words will move you forward in this exciting profession.

Lastly, if you are among the readers who don't quite understand the full gamut of what public relations entails, you will become more enlightened. I hope you'll be amused at times too.

The stories in this book are the ones that I am especially fond of. Many may be difficult to believe, but I assure you they are real. I couldn't have made them up! So I invite you to be a fly on the wall and travel into the never-boring arena of public relations as I professionally and personally experienced it. It was quite a journey. And I had an inside seat all the way.

I am eternally grateful,
Maxine Adler

By the time I joined the Adler Network in February 1996, I already had nearly two decades of public relations, advertising, and media experience under my belt. Nevertheless, Maxine Adler became an important mentor along my own career path. I immediately fit into the agency and became part of the Adler culture. Until I retired in 2014, I worked alongside this savvy PR icon—the grande dame of design and real estate-focused public relations in South Florida. We instantly developed a special relationship and a friendship based on mutual understanding, admiration, and respect. Together, we lived these stories and so many others.

Though small in size, Maxine was a powerhouse—a dynamic force filled with energy and ideas. She was tenacious and indefatigable. She always saw the big picture. I, on the other hand, gave her reality checks and provided the voice of reason. I pulled the details together and facilitated them. Our back-and-forth brainstorming and banter led to the birth of creative ideas and strategies. When she thought totally out of the box, I learned that almost anything was possible. More often than not, we were able to make what was seemingly unachievable actually happen. It could not have been any better than that.

Maxine knew a lot of people. And if she didn't know someone, she would say she did and then find a way to get to that person and make them an ally. Her network was far reaching and long lasting.

I hope that **my voice, interjected in italics here and in many of the stories that follow,** *will further your understanding of the unique bond that Maxine and I shared, one that we both believe benefited our cadre of clients—as well as our vast network of industry colleagues—in countless ways. We shouldered tremendous responsibilities and labored hard, but the rewards were worth it.*

Thanks for these memories,
Judy Goldstein

CHAPTER 1

When the Dust Settled

THE ODOR SURROUNDING ME WAS unidentifiable and inimitable. Not a burning smell like I had anticipated. Not medicinal, noxious, or awful. Just foreign to the senses. Gaseous. As soon as I first detected it, one of the thin elastic bands on my surgical mask began tugging uncomfortably over my left ear. But I didn't dare remove the mask. Not yet anyway. Instead, I instinctively adjusted it.

This was not one of those feigned disasters I had been involved in at Beth Israel Hospital in Passaic, New Jersey, back in the early seventies. That event had been designed to help us prioritize the order in which we treated victims. This event, on the other hand, was *real*.

Then I saw them. My husband, Owen, and the rest of our team. They were huddled together, barely visible to me, but nevertheless safe. I exhaled deeply, with both relief and gratitude.

Just seconds before, the ominous cloud of dust from the explosions had engulfed me and literally taken my breath away. Had there been a miscalculation in the direction and velocity of the wind? Maybe not. Perhaps this was how it was supposed to be. I was new to this, and no amount of advanced directives or meetings had prepared me for what I had just witnessed. This was probably a once-in-a-lifetime occurrence for most people. I knew how truly special it was, which made it easier to bear.

It wasn't until the air began to clear that I looked down at my clothing. Like everyone else's, it too was covered with a coat of thick gray dust. But we were okay, and that's what truly mattered.

Suddenly, I heard voices around me. Hundreds of them. Exhilarated. Then it came: the roaring applause. I felt proud to have been a part of something so big.

It was 2004 in South Florida, and I no longer was in the health care field. How had I gotten here?

I thought back to how it all began and smiled.

CHAPTER 2

The Beginning

MAXINE SCHWARTZ MET OWEN ADLER when she was eighteen years old in Passaic, New Jersey, where they both grew up. Eight years her senior, Owen was handsome, smart, outgoing, and the life of the party. He stole her heart and then gave her a wedding ring and a home—in addition to the confidence to believe she could do anything she set her mind to doing. He was her business partner as well as the love of her life. Even after his passing in 2015, he still is. Sixty years of an exceptional marriage and partnership are indelible.

That was the two of us. How truly blessed we were to have raised a wonderful family and built a successful business *together*. But before I get into that, let me tell you how Owen and I met. It is a story in its own right.

THE SOUND OF VIOLINS

Following my breakup with the star football player from my high school team, I filled much of my time in the summer of 1953 working at my parents' millinery shop in Passaic. It was named Maxine's after me, their first born. I answered the phone at Maxine's one day to discover it was Herman Taubman. He asked me out on a date because he had heard I was no longer dating Arnold. I wasn't really interested in Herman's invitation, but he coaxed me into accepting by telling me we'd be double dating with his best friend Owen Adler and Owen's girlfriend. I didn't know Owen Adler, nor did I particularly care. But he said Owen was a bundle of laughs.

On that Saturday evening, Herman and I joined the other couple at a fine dining establishment in nearby Millburn. I was seated between the two fellows. During the main course, Owen asked me to pass the salt. When I did, he held onto my hand a little too long. The same thing occurred when he asked me to pass the pepper. Then one of his legs softly brushed against mine. I was still in my teens and didn't know what to do. I did, however, know that something was going on. It sounds corny, but I swear that I heard violins! I was swept away.

When Owen's girlfriend excused herself to go "powder her nose," I followed her into the ladies' room. I don't know why. I never used public restrooms if I could avoid them. I'm still like that to this day.

While we were alone, the girlfriend confided in me.

"Tonight's the night." It was her way of telling me she was going to have sex with Owen for the first time. During the fifties, if a guy took a girl's virginity, he was likely to propose to her and then marry her. I guess she thought that sex would seal the deal.

But in my mind, I was thinking, "I don't think so, dear." I believed this even though she was positioning herself to be Owen's temptress later in the evening.

When we returned to the table, I experienced a repeat performance. Owen asked me to pass the cream and then the sugar. The touching continued. He couldn't help himself. As for me, those violins were now components in a full-fledged orchestra!

A few days later, Owen called and invited me to go out with him. It was July, and I was living with my parents in a lovely two-story home in suburban Passaic. At the time, my mother's mother—my *Bubbe* Hertz—was visiting us for one week. She did that every year, coming from Newark where she lived with my mom's kid sister, Evelyn, and Evelyn's four children. My grandmother had been born in Eastern Europe, migrated to the United States, and only spoke Yiddish.

My grandmother and mom were sitting in the backyard when Owen pulled up driving a red late-model Oldsmobile convertible.

Grandma asked my mother "Ver is das?" (Who is that?)

"Maxine haut a date," (Maxine has a date) answered Mom.

"Zi zol chasunh im!" (She should marry him!) insisted my grandmother. With her old-fashioned European mind-set, she thought that if you owned a car, you must be rich. As it turned out, Owen Adler was earning fifty dollars a week, a substantial sum of money back in those years.

With the "girlfriend" gone, Owen and I officially began our courtship. We became engaged in November 1953. Living in a small yet strong Jewish community, both sets of parents were ecstatic. Our moms and dads were involved in the local synagogues and known in our town. A matchmaker could not have done any better.

While I had been in high school, I talked about wanting to study psychology in college. But my guidance counselor told me that I cared too much about people and would become too emotionally involved with my patients. This would become an occupational hazard.

"But I want to be in a field where I can make a difference," I recall telling her.

"You can make a difference in other ways. I suggest that you study marketing." So I did.

I attended Farleigh Dickerson University and had taken advertising, print media, and some other marketing-related courses. Then after two years, in March 1954, I withdrew to get married. I wanted a family.

THE EARLY YEARS

After our son Jeffrey was born, I did volunteer work for local charities such as Women's American ORT and other nonprofits. I always liked the discussion group meetings more than the luncheons. I honestly didn't enjoy being around women unless they were my dear girlfriends. Owen was very dynamic, so I sat with him and his male friends quite often. I found their conversations far more interesting and stimulating.

One of the organizations took us on a group tour of the Greystone Park Psychiatric Hospital in Morris Plains, New Jersey. The historic building was beautiful, but when I entered and walked around, I was appalled to see so many patients overly medicated. Some had been restrained in their beds. The windows had bars over them. Seeing this broke my heart, so I abandoned my group and stormed into the administrator's office. I pointed out how warm and sunny it was outside.

"There are blue skies and sunshine! Why are these patients indoors, cooped up, instead of getting fresh air and enjoying nature? This is an injustice!"

Although I was enraged, the administrator simply paid me lip service. In those days, no one spoke about mental disorders. And there certainly was no such thing as people having *issues*.

After he blew me off, I left. I, however, suddenly wanted to right the wrongs in the health care industry. *That's* where I wanted to make a difference.

Fortunately, I discovered later that, starting from the mid sixties through the eighties, mental health was redirected toward deinstitutionalization. Individual states decided that many patients benefited more from living with their families while undergoing treatment. In addition, new medications made patients who had previously been considered dangerous now capable of living at home. In the seventies, Greystone was required to build a halfway house type of living environment. I was thrilled.

Yes. I wanted to pursue my dream of making a difference. On the other hand, I wanted to be a stay-at-home mom until Jeffrey started school. My own mother had worked for as long as I can remember, and I didn't understand why my friends' moms were at home baking cookies when *my* mom wasn't. At the same time, I was proud of my mom and her accomplishments in business. It wasn't until later, when I had a business of my own, that I realized how truly gratifying it could be for a woman to work outside the home.

Beth Israel Hospital

At the start of the seventies, I received a phone call from a gal I knew. I wasn't looking for a job, but that changed when she told me there was a position open as the director of volunteers at the not-for-profit Beth Israel Hospital. It was located in an inner city section of Passaic; nonetheless, my ears perked up. I went for an interview with David Wachs, the administrator. He told me that besides overseeing the volunteers, I would serve as the hospital's public information officer. The hospital needed information to get out to the media and to the public in the form of press releases and other materials respectively. I would also keep David organized and prepare him for his board meetings. He offered me a hundred dollars per week and a beeper because I would be on call 24-7. I made it clear that I must be available to my family if and when they needed me. When he agreed, I accepted the job.

"Only one hundred dollars a week? What were you thinking?" Owen questioned that evening. "You should have asked for more!"

At that time, the always-entrepreneurial Owen Adler owned a service station with his father. They also had relationships with a Pontiac car dealership and a car wash. Everyone helped each other. It was that kind of town. Owen was making a nice living, but who couldn't use a little extra money?

"Owen, one hundred dollars a week is *a lot* of money. Now we will be able to afford to put our son in summer camp and do more things for him."

I was thrilled. I loved my job and the wonderful hospital board members. They were the pillars of the Passaic community and knew Owen's parents and mine. They belonged to the same synagogues. My family belonged to Temple Emanuel; Owen's father, Saul Adler, was the president of Tifereth Israel.

I worked at Beth Israel Hospital for just over seven years. When I started, there were fifty volunteers. By the time I left, I had more than one thousand *serious* volunteers from all walks of life who helped the hospital's staff. I kept in touch with many of them over the years, even after I left that job.

Another accomplishment I am proud of is originating the idea for the Patient's Bill of Rights. I belonged to the New Jersey Hospital Association and brought my ideas to their meetings. Among other things, I wanted the doctors to speak to the family members of indigent patients on Medicaid, not just to the wives of the board of directors who had undergone surgery or had a procedure done. There needed to be equality among patients.

Later on, working with Beth Israel's new administrator, Ronald Milch, I helped select heads of the various departments. We faked city disasters for the hospital staff to triage victims to ensure that those victims would be treated according to their needs. I also started a hospice program in the hospital.

I truly enjoyed being involved in the health care field. Every chance I got, I ate lunch with the doctors in the hospital cafeteria. I was the only woman executive to do so. I was fascinated by their medical conversations.

During those years, no matter how hard I worked, it was important to me that my family ate dinner together, and ate well. I oftentimes marinated meat in the morning and cut up fresh vegetables. Then, when I came home—even if it was late, I made meals from scratch, such as beef rollatini, zuppa di pesce, eggplant parmigiana, stuffed veal chops, and "bumpy" chicken. My family never had Campbell's SpaghettiOs or Chef Boyardee anything. That's how the Adlers became a family of foodies. In fact, when Jeffrey was going away to sleep-away camp, I made him his ten favorite dishes before he left town. I usually did this on consecutive nights. He loved eating those meals, and I loved making them for him. He literally wolfed them down and licked his fingers so the taste lingered.

I also would follow that same tradition with my grandchildren who were living close by. As the years passed, my daughter-in-law, Honey, used my recipes to cook for her own family too. And, best of all, I would later come to see some of my granddaughters using those recipes for their families as well. Three generations enjoying Maxine Adler's home-cooked selections!

While working at Beth Israel, I experienced unwanted sexual "advances" for the first time in my life. A male colleague put his hand up my skirt. If I had told Owen about this, he would have killed the guy. So I never did. Fortunately, I was fast on my feet and quick to tell this colleague that I admired him, but this *cannot* happen. I was very direct about it. This occurred before the term "sexual harassment" was coined in the late seventies. Had there been harassment when this happened, I would have stopped it short just like I did. Being a happily married woman, I was hardly chaste. But I loved and was committed to my husband. I also was against fraternization in the work place. When I said "no," I meant business. No monkey business.

In those days, however, it was quite common for physicians and nurses to have sexual encounters in the operating rooms or supply closets, after their surgeries were finished for the day. I'm certain that this still happens today. The television series *Grey's Anatomy* is right on the mark.

One of my favorite memories was an event I planned for the hospital that piggybacked off a television show by broadcast TV host and producer David Susskind. His special had been called "Don't Get Sick in America."

I obtained Susskind's permission to plan an event, which also would be named "Don't Get Sick in America." It would attract professionals in the health care industry from New Jersey and New York. His mission had been to provide the first public awareness of the skyrocketing costs of health care. The system was broken (and, sadly, it still is). I wanted to get that message out as well. Like the television personality himself, I too wanted to find out who was at fault for the astronomical rise in costs and what could be done about it.

The event took place in February during the early seventies, on the same day that Roe v. Wade was being filibustered in the US Senate. I had reserved space to accommodate more than a thousand people at a motel in the Meadowlands, near Secaucus, New Jersey. I also had selected four categories of presenters: hospital administrators, physicians, insurance companies, and representatives from Congress. The event was heavily promoted through PSAs (public service announcements), which didn't cost anything. TV and radio stations aired them without charge. Also, I expected a large turnout of important media. This was *big* news.

On the day of *our* "Don't Get Sick in America," there was a major blizzard in the Northeast. The shop that was printing our event programs had burned down the night before. So, early that morning, the owner of the shop and I carried the typesetting and fonts to his competitor, who was able to complete the job for us. A finished printed program was then placed on the seat of each attendee, as I had originally planned. There were also electrical issues. When long extension cords were placed on the floor, I knew they could cause injury if someone should happen to trip over them. So I made sure that they were secured down with electrical tape. There were hundreds of minor details, and each one mattered.

Right before the event was to begin, Ronald Milch, Beth Israel Hospital's administrator, was suspected of having had a heart attack. He was placed onto a gurney and rushed from his office to the coronary care unit. He ended up being okay.

In spite of these problems, the event was a huge success. We had over eleven hundred people, including the participants, attendees, and the press.

I came out looking like a hero, especially because the *New York Times* featured the event on its *front page*. This was quite an achievement for a Jersey girl who hadn't finished college.

CHAPTER 3

Planting South Florida Roots

Northeast to Southeast

AROUND THE MID SEVENTIES, OWEN and I talked about moving our family down to Florida. By then my dad had passed away, and my mom had remarried. She and her wonderful new husband lived in Bal Harbour.

In 1976 Owen went to Florida to begin looking into businesses. This was the only time since we had gotten married that we spent a week without sleeping in the same bed. On his first trip away from me, Owen stayed with a cousin. On subsequent trips, I went along, and we stayed together at a hotel near the Fort Lauderdale/Hollywood International Airport. This was around the time that I would soon resign from the hospital.

Owen considered a few different manufacturing businesses but had his heart set on starting a new company, Bagel-O's of Florida, which would produce bagel chips. This was a unique concept at the time. Initially, we relocated our family to a rental townhome in Inverrary in Lauderhill while our home was being built in Plantation. After having created the Bagel-O's name as well as displays, and with a trademark pending, Owen opened a store in Lauderdale Lakes. He bought freshly baked bagels from the popular Marian's Bagel Shop in Plantation, and then he cut them into chips with a special machine. This was a real challenge because no two bagels were ever alike. It was difficult to make the chips consistent. Yet my dedicated husband kept trying to perfect the method.

Our son Jeffrey had just graduated from Syracuse University, and he began working with Owen to develop the Bagel-O's brand and open up markets across the country. I worked in the store with them on weekends. I was also a shill. I stood at the checkout counters in Publix, Winn-Dixie, and Albertson's supermarkets and asked where I could find Bagel-O's. I made sure my voice was heard. Someone would answer, "Sorry. We don't carry Bagel-O's." And I told them, "You should! They are the next best thing to sliced bread."

I decided to find a job at a hospital, but none of the hospitals in South Florida recognized the value of hiring a PR specialist. I had thought this would be a piece of cake. I went to visit each one, carrying the *New York Times'* front cover story about my "Don't Get Sick in America" event, thinking, "I'm Maxine Adler. I'm here. Hire me!" Easy, right? Wrong. What I had thought would be a cinch turned out to be impossible at that time.

I also wanted to plant roots in the local community, especially for the sake of my family. That's why I knocked on the door of the Soref Jewish Community Center on the Perlman Family Campus, situated on West Sunrise Boulevard in Plantation, and offered to do pro bono work. This occurred right after I had heard that there were signs of anti-Semitism in the neighborhood, something which I had never experienced. The Baer and Schagrin families *(think furniture* and *wine)*, among others, were very active at the JCC during the time that I helped out. We all wanted to contribute to the welfare of the entire community.

Concurrently, the Adlers began making friends.

First Florida Job

My first paid job in South Florida was as the director of communications for Susan Lachance Interior Design. I worked at Susan's office, which was less than a ten-minute drive from my home. She gave me a salary and a company car to use.

Susan had a wonderful demeanor and a staff of other talented designers. Among them were Curtis House, who had been a designer for General Mica, and Debra Juliano, to name two of them.

At the time, Susan's specialty was the commercial interiors of banks. Her client list grew when the bankers themselves retained her services to create the interiors of their homes. She also furnished the commercial spaces for Ryder Truck Rental locations in South Florida, as well as designed the interiors for the head of that company's residence.

Lachance designs, which ranged from traditional and transitional to contemporary and metropolitan, were quite notable. But there was something more. Not only was Susan a woman with a creative flair, but she also had built an amazing business in a male-dominated profession. So I reached out to *Florida Trend* magazine and convinced them that Susan and her firm were worth writing about. The magazine assigned a writer who soon went with Susan and me to visit every project she had completed. I think it might have taken us two or three days. *Florida Trend* provided a helicopter too, so that the sites could be seen and photographed from the air. We were hoping for a cover story. This was a big deal for Susan, the magazine and me until…I was at home preparing dinner one night and received a call from the magazine's publisher. He introduced himself and said he had bad news to tell me.

"We had to kill the article."

At the time, I was holding a marinated chicken in a flimsy aluminum pan. I set it down on the kitchen counter or else I would have dropped it. I can still smell the garlic, olive oil, and lemon juice to this day!

"Why? Why do you have to kill the story?" I asked.

"Because we found out that Lionel Reifler, Susan Lachance's husband, is a convicted felon."

Between 1968 and 1976, Lionel Reifler reportedly had six felony convictions for crimes including securities fraud, tax evasion, the sale of unregistered securities, and the operation of an unregistered brokerage firm.

I wasn't certain whether or not Lionel was an actual owner in his wife's design business, but he appeared to be quite involved with its daily operations.

After the shock wave wore off and I hung up the phone, I immediately called our close friend, who was also our attorney. Alan Werksman advised me to go to Susan's office first thing the next morning, use my office key to enter, and put my letter of resignation on Susan's desk, along with that key, and the key to the car she had let me drive. I did exactly what he told me to do.

I found out later that Lionel made every employee of the firm take a lie detector test after I had left. He thought that I had contacted them after my resignation and that I intended to tell the secrets of the company to the world. I had not contacted them, nor did I intend to let anything out of the bag—including the cat.

Since I had developed relationships with many of the designers, *they* contacted me in the future. We kept in touch. Some became clients of the PR agency that Owen and I soon founded.

More than thirty years later, I ran into Susan at an event at the One Thousand Ocean condominium property in Boca Raton. The new property was a client of ours. We had invited top South Florida designers, knowing that they had upscale clients who could afford these ultra-luxe residences. If a designer's client decided to purchase another residence, then it was likely the designer would again be retained to create the new interiors. And the budget would be big because One Thousand Ocean was for the very rich.

When Susan and I spoke at that event, she was charming and very friendly. Not long after that, she invited me to a gathering at her home in St. Andrews Country Club, which she shared with her *second* husband. It was a reunion of all of the people she had employed through the years, in addition to her current staff.

Susan Lachance was the first of many interior designers I would represent. While Curtis House was still working for Susan, this consummate and tireless professional said he had something to discuss with Owen and me. So we took him out to dinner. We met at Nick's Fish Market at One Boca Place on Glades Road. I can still remember that restaurant and the food we ate. (I told you that I was a foodie!) It was during appetizers that Curtis told us he wanted to leave Susan's firm and strike out on his own.

"I have no money to pay you. Will you still represent me?"

We didn't have to think twice about it and agreed. We admired Curtis and recognized his potential. He went on to establish Direct Interiors in Delray Beach, and our relationship with him lasted many years,

And years after that, Debra Juliano, who had been on both Susan's and Curtis's design teams, became our client when she started her own company in Boca Raton.

BIRTH OF A BUSINESS

After the Susan Lachance debacle, I asked myself, "What do I want to do with the rest of my life?" Not long after that, Owen and Jeffrey decided to give up on Bagel-O's and close it down. They realized that it would never become the enterprise they had wanted it to be because, seemingly at the time, there was no slicing equipment to keep up with the national demand they had created.

While this was happening, I started meeting some members of the local press. One individual, in particular, impressed and influenced me. After talking with John Degroot, a Pulitzer Prize–winning journalist at the *Sun-Sentinel*, I realized that I still wanted to interact with the media. But perhaps do it for a number of different clients at the same time.

As a result, Owen and I made a joint decision to go into the public relations field together. We started working from our home office in Plantation in 1978. After coming up with the name, the Adler Group, our attorney Alan Werksman did a search and told us that the name had already been taken by Michael Adler, who was in the real estate business. Alan asked us for another name, and I spontaneously came up with the Adler Network. Owen liked it, and we both thought it would make our start-up business appear to be bigger than it was. Image was as important to us as it was to other businesses—and we eventually applied this thinking to our future clients.

I was the president and Owen was the executive vice president, but he became my partner in every way. We decided that he should handle financial matters because he knew I would "give away the store." (Yet I sometimes did.) An expert negotiator, my husband also would hire vendors early on, while I would take charge of day-to-day client service. Our vendors admired and respected Owen, and he always paid their invoices as quickly as possible.

I began cultivating more relationships with the media, and it was Charlyne Varkonyi-Schaub, the home and design editor at the *Sun-Sentinel*, who referred me to Estelle Nemoy. She was Charlyne's best friend and a writer. Estelle became our first writer. I went to her residence, discussed the content for the press releases and feature stories that I needed her to write, and then picked them up from her. There was no such thing as Word documents, digital files, or e-mail back then. Everything was a "hard copy." This worked well for us, and Estelle continued writing for us for approximately a year after we opened our first office, which was on Federal Highway near Commercial Boulevard in Fort Lauderdale.

Then in the early eighties, we relocated to the Cypress Creek/I-95 area of Fort Lauderdale. Owen had struck an amazing deal, leasing a huge amount of square footage for the Adler Network in a new modern office building. We wanted our space to be drop-dead gorgeous, comparable to that of an agency one would find in Manhattan. Since interior designer Roy Sklarin was among our first clients, we worked with him to create an environment that was very impressive. It incorporated dramatic black-and-white marble floors, and black, silver, gray, chrome and glass furniture. Later we adorned a large entry wall with a display of covers of national and international magazines in which we had gotten our clients prominent editorial coverage. We called it our "Wall of Fame."

Although our agency had a diverse roster of clients in a wide range of industries over the years, we seemed best suited to luxury real estate development and design. Helping to generate positive exposure for residential and commercial developers, custom builders, architects, and interior designers became our strong suit, and our reputation in those sectors grew. During my frequent visits to new construction sites, I proudly wore a hardhat like a crown atop my voluminous French twist hairdo. I ruined business suits, silk blouses, and dozens of pairs of high-heeled pumps without a complaint…and without charging our clients for the cost of new ones.

Our firm never entered PR industry award competitions (although we *did* submit award-winning design and real estate award entries for our clients). We had neither the time nor the inclination to do this for ourselves. We received our rewards from seeing our clients succeed. We also had portfolios and file cabinets bulging with press clippings we had gotten for them, which brought us great satisfaction. Showing some of that press coverage to prospective clients convinced most of them to retain our services for themselves.

For about twenty years, the Adler Network offered advertising among its services. We had an in-house graphics department producing print ads, newsletters, direct mail pieces, and invitations. The time, however, eventually came when we began focusing solely on public relations, marketing, and consulting. That was because some of our clients already had ad agencies on retainer. We wanted to avoid any conflicts of interest with those advertising firms. We met with them regularly during client meetings to ensure there would be a cohesive message. Consequently, we enjoyed a nonthreatening working relationship with advertising firms such as Creative Directors, Beber Silverstein, Marc USA, Ronin Advertising, Soffer Advertising, Green Advertising, Len Dugow and Associates, Cotton and Company, and others. Even then, in addition to creating press releases, feature stories, speeches, letters, and ghost-written guest columns, *our* "PR" functions included *writing* copy for advertorials (paid articles), newsletters, and event invitations.

I personally preferred public relations to advertising. In my opinion, editorial content was far more powerful than a paid advertisement. And whenever the Adler Network was able to get a lengthy feature story about a client published, we would tell that client what the cost would have been if he or she had to *pay* for that amount of space. Most readers perceive the "written word" to be much more credible. I think this credibility factor is the same for radio listeners and television viewers when they hear a news report or interview. It's just not the same as a thirty- or sixty-second *paid* commercial.

Also, through our numerous client affiliations, we were privileged to have worked with high-profile real estate planning, marketing, and new construction sales companies: The Sunshine Group (Florida), International Sales Group (ISG), Premier Sales Group, and Corcoran Sunshine Marketing Group. We also are happy to include real estate marketing consultant Candace Jorritsma in this group.

Over the years, I never felt guilty about the long hours I worked because Owen did too. We ate our meals, entertained clients, and traveled together, as well as shared a bed and pillow talk each night. Together we settled into a satisfying and sometimes very exciting family, business, and social life.

Owen was an extraordinary husband and partner. He always encouraged and supported me in business, and our personal and professional values, as well as the culture of the Adler Network, were in sync. We only argued if I charged clients too little, or if I continued working for them after they hadn't paid their bills for several months!

In 1996, Judy Goldstein—the sister I never had—became part of the Adler team. More about that in chapter 16.

Because Judy, Owen, and I had moved to Boca Raton in the mid nineties, years later we moved our business to the Clint Moore Road/Congress Avenue intersection. It was much more convenient for us. Plus, many real estate developers and builders whom we were representing had projects located north of us.

In a nutshell, that's an abbreviated history of the Adler Network. But I assure you that our experiences over the years were far more than blueprints, bricks and mortar, fabric, and color boards. They involved real people with different and sometimes conflicting personalities. It became a delicate balancing act, which we were able to fine tune as the years flew by.

And now, let the stories begin!

CHAPTER 4

The Silver Fox

ROY SKLARIN WAS ONE OF many gifted interior designers that our agency served over our many years in business. Owen and I were still working out of our home in Plantation when we began representing Roy in the early eighties. Our relationship lasted about a decade.

His office was on the top floor of an office building on Federal Highway, near Commercial Boulevard in Fort Lauderdale. He told us there was space available on a lower floor, which we subsequently leased. Having the Adler Network's office in the same building as our client's suite was quite a convenience. Plus, Roy helped us with the décor.

At that time in South Florida, most designers were creating traditional or transitional interiors. But not Roy. He was a contemporary design genius.

In addition to his skill as a designer, there was another thing about Roy that no one could deny. It was his flamboyance. He was, quite literally, addicted to jewelry, furs, and exotic cars. No drugs, although he did sometimes overdose on White Russian cocktails. At times, he wore a diamond ring on every finger. He owned full-length sables, minks, chinchillas, and other furs. And how he loved his cars! He might have had as many as seven automobiles stored in garages when he was going through his car phase. Every car had a black exterior and a black interior, even though in those days it was rare to see a black automobile in Florida because of the heat.

Another amazing thing about Roy was that he could be broke on Monday and rich again on Tuesday. You had to love the guy, and Owen and I became very close friends of his. So close that when his mother passed away, we made arrangements for the funeral service, burial, and *shiva*.

While we were helping build Roy's brand in South Florida, he created the interiors of a home in Palm Beach belonging to Leonard and Sunny Sessa. Leonard operated Leonard's of Great Neck, a successful company that set the standard for the catering industry. Following his divorce from his first wife, he married Sunny.

Since most of us don't know what goes on behind closed doors, I will tell you that their master bedroom had mirrors on the ceilings. And the centerpiece of their living room was a Lucite piano that Liberace had designed and played. There were only two pianos of this kind at the time, so Roy bought the second one and put it into his own trendy condo penthouse in Fort Lauderdale.

The Sessas liked very fine modern art. Therefore, a color transparency (photograph) of one of their art pieces was given to Aggie Ash, the publisher of *Palm Beach Life* magazine, after I had interested her in doing a cover story about designer Roy Sklarin and the Sessa residence. I also had given Aggie additional photos of the home's interiors for publication. A magazine needs a vertical shot for its front cover, and the only vertical shot I had was of that particular piece of exotic art. A day later, Aggie called me.

"Maxine, we're definitely going to do this story, but I can't possibly use *that* photo on the cover. In fact, I may not be able to use it at all."

The photo she referred to was a depiction of an elephant with a huge trunk *and* a huge penis. It looked like the animal had a hard-on! Needless to say, I immediately called back the professional photographer, who scurried to take a vertical shot of something else in the Sessa residence to replace the one that had been rejected.

Roy was also an accomplished designer of luxury yacht interiors. Through the Adler Network, he forged a relationship with our clients Bob and Sharon Roscioli of the Roscioli Yachting Center in Fort Lauderdale. Roy subsequently was commissioned to create the interiors for many of their customers' yachts.

On one occasion, one of those yachts was used in an episode of *Miami Vice*, the popular television crime drama about two undercover detectives. I didn't watch the show, so I really didn't know what it was about or who starred in it. All I had heard was that the cocaine boom of the eighties in Miami provided inspiration for the show's storylines (i.e., drugs and murder). I also had heard that many of the scenes were filmed on Biscayne Bay or out on the ocean.

I was put in contact with Michael Mann, the show's producer, and took my instructions from him and his production crew. On the day of the scheduled filming, I was on the yacht with Owen. When they would begin filming, we would move out of camera range. Meanwhile, we were on the deck waiting. A scruffy-looking guy came aboard. He wore a rumpled white linen suit, had a head of messy, windblown hair, and a thick five o'clock shadow. I was a bit put off. Was this a mistake, or was this guy supposed to be here?

"Excuse me. Who are you?" I asked him.

Owen immediately jabbed his elbow into my ribs. Then he whispered to me, "That's Don Johnson. He plays the role of Sonny Crockett." He was the star of the series! I was shocked!

Soon his co-star Philip Michael Thomas, who played Ricardo "Rizo" Tubbs, boarded the vessel along with NFL basketball center Bill Russell. At six foot ten, Russell towered over everyone else and had to bend down in order to fit into the yacht's salon. He was playing a judge turned bad because of gambling debts. The first airing was during the show's second season on NBC, in an episode called "The Fix" in March 1986. The yacht's TV debut was a hit.

Because it was considered cool to be associated with this widely recognized TV series, we maintained contact with the production company and suggested locations to them for future episodes. All of those locations were on the water, including numerous restaurants with docks. If the location was selected and agreed to participate, *Miami Vice* would pay them a location fee. Of course, *we* weren't paid anything for our recommendations!

Although Roy was very successful as a designer in this market, the bottom fell out when he started to have very serious financial difficulties. Consequently, he decided to move his business to California. This literally occurred overnight.

Because we respected Roy's talents, Owen forgave the money Roy owed to us and agreed that we'd continue representing him after his relocation to Los Angeles. It didn't take long before Roy gained a reputation as being a "designer for the stars" in his new milieu. With his creativity and resources, he also began making furniture adaptations. They weren't considered *knock-offs* by any means. If a bed in a furniture showroom cost $3,000, Roy's redesign would be pricier. No one seemed to care.

Owen and I took the red eye to Los Angeles at least once a month for years, during which times we cultivated, and then maintained, friendships with the editors and publishers of several design magazines being produced in that market. I was able to get Roy some great feature stories in those publications.

Relationships with the media matter. They are a PR professional's life blood.

One article, in *Designer's West* magazine, was about the home of Max Dauer, owner of Florida Medical Center (hospital) in Fort Lauderdale. It sat on an entire square block in Beverly Hills. Roy's client was a collector with walls and walls showcasing Tiffany glass. I remember this vividly because, during my visit to this house, there was an earthquake! This was the first (and last) time I ever experienced one. Aside from being frightened, I watched in horror as the Tiffany objets d'art shook and slid around. Fortunately, none had broken.

After Roy went to Los Angeles, he designed the interiors of Carol Connors's residence. The singer and songwriter was best known as the lead vocalist on the Teddy Bears' 1958 single "To Know Him Is to Love Him," written by Phil Spector. Carol also cowrote "Gonna Fly Now," the popular theme song for the movie *Rocky*.

Marilyn McCoo and Billy Davis were among Roy's high-profile clients too. The husband-and-wife team had formed the 5th Dimension, which became one of the most admired R&B singing groups during the sixties and seventies. Owen and I met them, and the couple was quite taken by us. I don't really know why.

As Roy was putting the finishing touches on the furnishings for their home, Marilyn and Billy asked us to go with them to assist in picking out a toilet seat. I guess they liked our style! So there we were, in various plumbing supply stores, watching these two performers and recording artists squatting down on a number of different toilet seats—wearing their clothes, of course. They apparently knew what felt comfortable, but they wanted us to weigh in on which toilet seat was the most aesthetically pleasing. I'm not kidding you. This *really* happened.

Furthermore, during the time that Roy was our client, I had the great pleasure of meeting the Cargill Macmillan Jrs. Their primary residence was in Minnesota, where the huge, privately held global corporation Cargill Inc. was headquartered. The company fed the world with everything from beef and turkey to grain and salt. The conglomerate also was involved with cotton, steel, energy, financial services, and more.

The Macmillan Jrs. owned a condominium in Palm Springs that Roy had furnished. Cargill, a multibillionaire, and his beautiful wife Donna were as nice and as hospitable as they could be. Because I had interested *Town & Country* magazine in featuring their condo in one of its issues, a writer, a photographer, and I spent a weekend with this couple. Donna was very knowledgeable about fine art, and she knew all of the details about their $20 million art collection. But what impressed me the most was how down to earth Cargill was. This fabulously wealthy man was the most delightful person I had ever met. No pretense at all. Although *Forbes* magazine included him on its list of the four hundred richest Americans, you'd never know he was a Cargill agribusiness heir.

One day, when Cargill went to pick up lunch for us, I drove with him to the community's clubhouse in his run-of-the-mill American-made Mercury Sable. We brought back salads, sandwiches, and beverages. When we arrived at the condo, we discovered that Donna had gone to the trouble of making iced tea. Not wanting to insult or offend her, he put the bought beverages into the refrigerator and served us the tea. And we drank it all, considering the temperature in Palm Springs had reached an unbearable one hundred ten degrees.

Another time, when I had called Cargill, he answered. He must have had a phone in his shower.

"Hello, Maxine. I'm in the shower. I'll call you back."

He did. Right away. He was quite the gentleman.

During our time with Roy Sklarin, Owen and I sometimes went with him and his partner Michael to the most famous gay club in Los Angeles. My husband and I didn't care about anyone else's sexual preference. Being open minded broadened our world. And it especially broadened mine. I dressed well and was considered to have a good figure. I wasn't conceited, but I was confident that men thought of me as being attractive and somewhat "hot." Yes, in that club, for the first time in my life, not a single male looked at me. Everyone looked at Owen instead.

I recall the night when Michael came out of the restroom and returned to our table.

"Everybody wants to know who the 'Silver Fox' is at Roy's table."

Owen had a head of gorgeous thick silvery-white hair. After that, Owen became known as the Silver Fox. That nickname stuck, not only in California but in Florida too.

Although we parted ways after about a decade, Roy went on to develop an international presence. His firm is still based in Beverly Hills and the Roy Sklarin Interiors' website displays the March 1990 *Town & Country* cover story "At Home with the Cargill Macmillan Jrs." that I just mentioned.

Postscript: We came a long way from representing Susan Lachance and then Roy Sklarin. Over the years, we went on to represent many other design talents: Curtis House (Direct Interiors), Ted Fine (Fine Decorators), Alene Workman (Alene Workman Interior Design), Maura Taft (Maura Taft Associates), Debra Juliano (Debra Juliano Interior Design), Perla Lichi (Perla Lichi Design), Robert Weinstein (Weinstein Design Group), Judy Howard

(J/Howard Design), and Louis Shuster (Shuster Design Associates), to name a few. This doesn't include the many other designers whom we promoted because they had completed furnished model residences for our developer clients. Likewise, we served high-end home furnishings retailers Roche Bobois and Robb & Stucky, as well as Judith Norman and several other showrooms at DCOTA (Design Center of the Americas).

This wasn't necessarily by design. We just had a knack for it.

CHAPTER 5

For What It's Worth

WORTH AVENUE, THAT ICONIC STREET between the Atlantic Ocean and Lake Worth on the famed island of Palm Beach, needs little introduction. Standard Oil mogul Henry Flagler and architect Addison Mizner both have been credited with transforming the four-block stretch into a global shopping destination. Called the Rodeo Drive of Florida because of its upscale shops offering internationally recognized and locally inspired brands, it has panache unrivalled in the state, except perhaps for the Bal Harbour Shops.

THE ESPLANADE

Having knowledge of retailing helped me when we were hired by the Goodman Company in the later part of 1979 to plan the grand opening of the Esplanade. The new, two-story retail complex was located on the eastern end of Worth Avenue, at 150 Worth, where Worth intersects South County Road. The elegant structure still features Saks Fifth Avenue as its original anchor store. Saks had first opened elsewhere on the avenue in 1926 when it was the only SFA outside of New York City.

Following the demolition of what had been the Ocean View Hotel on the site, developer Murray Goodman broke ground on the Esplanade in 1978. Upon its completion in 1980, Owen and I were front and center for the opening of its first phase.

Architect Gene Lawrence was considered one of Palm Beach's most important designers. He and his Lawrence Group Architects designed the Esplanade.

His credits would also include Neiman Marcus, Salvatore Ferragamo, Cartier, Trillion, the Palm Beach Park Centre office building on Royal Palm Way, and Café L'Europe. Lawrence's signature would also be reflected on residential buildings at Sloan's Curve, The Sun and Surf, L'Ermitage of Palm Beach, The Reef, The Regency of Palm Beach, Il Lugano, and Bellaria. *Both Il Lugano by Ceebraid Signal, and Bellaria by Premier Palm Beach LP would become clients of the Adler Network years later.*

Designed to be a unique, all-day shopping experience, the open-air Esplanade was poised to attract locals, vacationers, celebrities, and royalty in much the same way that individual shops along the avenue had been doing since they began opening in the twenties. Along with being the introduction to Worth Avenue, the Esplanade was expected to be the be-all-end-all shopping and dining destination of the Palm Beaches—a veritable oasis for the well heeled.

The new complex had a luxurious entrance with a fountain and a grand staircase leading up to the second level. That was the inspiration for a fashion show that would be part of the black-tie grand opening. Because Emilio Pucci was one of the original tenants, I reached out to the acclaimed Florentine Italian designer and asked him to be the star of the evening and the commentator for the show, which would feature his popular fashions. I could already envision models on the upstairs catwalk as they descended the staircase dressed in his colorful signature geometric prints.

During the fifties and sixties, Pucci prints exemplified a designer's successful transition from haute couture to ready-to-wear. Emilio's runway and runway-inspired collections had been worn by Marilyn Monroe, Sophia Loren, Jackie Kennedy, Helen Gurley Brown, and Jacqueline Susann, to name of few of his celebrity customers. Even Braniff Airlines had commissioned the fashion designer to create uniforms for its flight attendants (who, then, were all females referred to as stewardesses or air hostesses). He made everything from kaleidoscopic swirling-print convertible dresses to bubble-like helmets that protected an attendant's perfect hairdo from rain while she walked from the terminal, onto the tarmac, and into the airplane. Focusing on efficiency as well as fashion, part of the uniforms were interchangeable and could be removed or altered during flights to adjust between day and night. Emilio Pucci created six collections for Braniff between 1965 and 1974, and the wardrobes were referred to as the "air strip." The fashion statement was in keeping with Braniff's advertising tagline, "The End of the Plain Plane."

Although Emilio was not a young man at the time of the Esplanade's grand opening, he agreed to participate, and he never disappointed us. On the contrary, he dazzled us, the Goodman Company, and the pedigreed guests whom we had invited to attend. They were the Who's Who of the Palm Beach Social Register, including some of the area's most philanthropic couples. We had access to mailing lists from the shops at the Esplanade, in addition to lists from the other stores along the fabled avenue.

On that same evening, Lidia and Norbert Goldner opened their Café L'Europe at the Esplanade. From the first time that well-dressed Palm Beach epicures and style makers entered that European-style dining establishment, it became the finest restaurant on the island and perhaps in the entire county. (In 1995, the Goldners relocated Café L'Europe to the corner of South County Road and Brazilian Avenue.)

As guest of honor for the evening's festivities, Emilio personally greeted everyone. What astounded me is that many of the women either wore a Pucci design or had a piece of Pucci clothing folded up in their handbags, which they showed to him. The fabric never wrinkled. You could fold, roll, or crumple it, then put it on, and still look pristine. It was ideal for traveling, and the majority of guests at the grand opening were indeed jetsetters.

Emilio had remarkable recall. He seemed to remember every woman who had visited his European salon and what she had purchased. He would say, "Hello, Mrs. (whatever her name was). I remember that you bought that blouse in 1969. You were with your husband. You liked one fabric; he liked another. So he insisted that you buy both."

For the fashion show portion of the evening, Emilio had personally selected the models, one more stunning than the next. I watched him pinch and pat each model's *tuchas* (rear end) as they were about to begin their walk. But it was not in the way a dirty old man would do it. The designer was highly respected and admired in the fashion world, so I suppose that gesture was just part of what he was known to do.

The day before, I had picked the designer up at the airport upon his arrival and took him to the Breakers in Palm Beach. After our event ended, Owen drove Emilio back to the hotel. I stayed behind at the Esplanade, as I did at *every* event venue, to ensure that all of the guests had left and the vendors had cleaned up and "broom swept" the floors. I never left any of our events until this was done.

When Owen returned to the Esplanade to pick me up, he was grinning from ear to ear. He told me that he and Emilio had thoroughly enjoyed each other's company. They conversed on a number of subjects and exchanged jokes as if they had been friends for a zillion years. It was a wonderful experience for Owen to have had.

The entire evening exuded style, taste, and class because that's how people did things on Palm Beach Island, and still do.

Our agency also had been hired by the Steinberg family who had expanded their South Florida retail business into the Esplanade. They had two stores on the second level. One sold high-end fashions; the other offered exquisite home accessories and giftware such as Baccarat crystal. We wanted to give their stores a boost by letting prospective customers know that these shops carried the same, similar, or even more unique items than they could find at a department store. Our challenge was to change the mentality of buyers in order to get them away from where they were accustomed to shopping and into the Steinbergs' stores.

Part of what I learned from being involved with the Esplanade was that many women didn't just stop by to browse or shop. They didn't simply buy "off the rack." They had a relationship with the shop's manager, buyer, or salesperson. They'd receive a phone call inviting them into the shop whenever new merchandise they might like came in. It could be something fabulous in their size or favorite color, or a gown that would be perfect for an upcoming family wedding or black-tie charity ball. There were very personal relation-ships involved in this world that I had never before lived in.

I also was privy to a story circulating around Saks Fifth Avenue in the Esplanade. I don't know whether it was gossip or the truth. But it was inter-esting and shocking at the same time. I was told that Rose Kennedy would purchase an evening gown for a Saturday night gala. Her photo would be taken by the *Shiny Sheet* (*aka* the *Palm Beach Daily News*) on that night and then appear in the popular glossy newspaper on Sunday. Rose Kennedy would come back to Saks Fifth Avenue on Monday, say she had never worn the gown, and return it. They allowed this because of who she was. I also heard that she did the same thing with bathing suits and lingerie! But this esteemed society woman and matriarch of the Kennedy clan was still well regarded. She also was a good customer when she did *not* return the merchandise.

Planning and coordinating the opening for the Esplanade's initial phase was a terrific and gratifying experience. After that, the development of the shopping complex would continue for the next two decades. Top-tier-brand shops like Pucci, Gucci, Louis Vuitton, and Tory Burch eventually joined other venerated fashion boutiques, as well as high-end accessory and giftware stores, fine jewelers, health and beauty salons, restaurants, a real estate office, and yacht brokerage firm. In 2000, specialty retailer Neiman Marcus opened across the street, at 151 Worth Avenue, adding to the center's draw. In 2006, a Starbucks opened at the Esplanade. To my knowledge, it is the only Starbucks on the island.

In 2010 a renovation restored and preserved the elegance of Worth Avenue for shoppers the world over to enjoy. Before that, in 2004, the Esplanade was renamed 150 Worth. Customers, however, continued to call it by its original name, and tenants requested that it revert back to its original moniker. So 150 Worth became the Esplanade again in 2015.

To me, Palm Beach and Worth Avenue are all about tradition. So I think that maintaining the original name was a very smart thing to do.

If it ain't broke, don't fix it.

CHAPTER 6
On the Waterfront

I GOT MY SEA LEGS while representing the Roscioli family. In marine lingo, the popular catchphrase means the ability to withstand the constant rolling and pitching of a boat to avoid motion sickness, or jelly legs, once back on land.

The Rosciolis were a great bunch: Bob, his wife Sharon, and their kids Robert Jr. and Heather. They were also great clients who taught us all about the boating industry, how big that industry is in South Florida, and the mentality of boat owners. As an example, we learned that the moment owners purchase a large yacht, they begin looking for the next upgrade.

The Adler Network was able to generate a lot of great publicity for their two marine companies—the Roscioli Yachting Center and Donzi by Roscioli International, located on State Road 84 overlooking the New River in Fort Lauderdale. We were initially hired in the early eighties to promote the yachting center. Then, after Bob bought the Donzi yacht line, we continued to work together. It was a terrific team relationship, and we went on to do some really interesting things, including events to establish the Donzi by Roscioli brand, as well as fundraisers with celebrities to benefit local youth.

The Roscioli story is a success story if there ever was one. Bob had his start in the marine industry as an apprentice at an early age. After graduating from high school in 1961, he looked for odd jobs. He was on the docks, working on anything he could get his hands on. He then found some work at a shipyard in Fort Lauderdale earning $1.10 an hour. He was prepping boats for painting, but they wouldn't let him paint, even though he wanted to learn how. After nine months of working hard, Bob asked for a dime raise. He didn't get the raise or his next paycheck. He had been fired.

"What did I do wrong? All I asked for was a ten cents an hour raise," he said to his boss. "I would have taken a nickel. I've been prepping for nine months and doing a good job."

"Well, ahhhh, you *asked* for a raise," he was told.

That was the day that changed Bob's life.

He then went on his own and got as many jobs as he could, while making $1.50 an hour, which was good money back in the sixties. Soon he was earning $2.00 an hour.

Next he had the opportunity to work for a very wealthy man who was in the horse business. He owned a one-hundred-five-footer (yacht, not horse!). It had been an air-and-sea rescue boat, but after spending $500,000 on it at a shipyard, it became one of the largest yachts in Broward County. That was like spending $10 million today. The last thing that had to be done was some work on the bottom. While raising the yacht up, the lift broke. The yacht fell over, knocking four large holes into one of her wooden sides. Bob was fortunate enough to meet the yacht's captain, who then hired him to do some maintenance and interior painting. Bob did the work on the North Fork of the New River. After many months, he found a spot at Striker Marine to help the captain of the yacht complete the repairs. When the project was finished, the captain and owner brought Bob another large yacht to work on. Following the completion of both of those projects, Bob seriously started to develop his career in the yachting business. The year was 1963.

Bob developed a revolutionary high-quality painting technique and product that no one else in the country knew about. With a lot of fortitude and sweat equity, Bob went house to house wherever there were canals in Fort Lauderdale, knocking on doors to get jobs cleaning and varnishing the boats owned by local residents. They were impressed with his exceptional work. He had mastered brush painting and then spray painting, which was unknown locally. He ran his company, Roscioli Yacht Refinishing, in the same location at Striker Marine for nineteen years and had thirty-five people working for him.

When Bob heard that I-595 was coming through and intersecting State Road 84, he realized he had to relocate, but he didn't know where to go. Then an opportunity came up, and he seized it. That opportunity was a full-service shipyard called Admiralty, which was closed at the time. He struck a deal with the new owner to lease the yard, with an option to buy. Bob leased for one and a half years and then purchased the property in 1982. He also changed his company name from Roscioli Yacht Refinishing to Roscioli Yachting Center that same year.

In 1986, Bob became a dealer for Donzi Marine Corp, owned by Dick Genth and John Staples. A year later, he bought the rights to Donzi's large boat division of luxury sportfishing yachts, as well as its factory in Bradenton, Florida, where he continues to build them.

Bob Roscioli became a legend in the megabucks world of megayachts. His experience and technical expertise contributed to a standard of excellence in custom yacht building, yacht repair, restoration, outfitting, and maintenance that is difficult to match. Through the years, he grew a business that caters to some of the most affluent boat owners around the globe. Now that the Roscioli children are grown, they too are working with him and Sharon.

Back in the eighties, I thought it would be mutually beneficial to introduce the Rosciolis to interior designer Roy Sklarin. After I did, Roy—who would later become the owner of a large yacht himself—was commissioned to design the interiors of several yachts that had been purchased by Roscioli customers. Roy's designs were fabulous and very "over the top," incorporating opulent materials such as fine woods, silk, and Lucite, as well as a lot of mirrors.

The Rosciolis, their vice president Tom Glass, Roy, Owen, and I went out socially quite often. I recall one humorous incident that occurred when we were together at the posh Beverly Hilton Hotel in Los Angeles. We were seated in the hotel's restaurant, and all of us had ordered eggs Benedict. When the waiter arrived carrying the platters on a large tray, he accidentally bumped into Owen, causing all of the eggs to slide off the tray onto Owen's shoulder and down his entire back. His sport jacket was a mess. The manager quickly responded, took the jacket, and had it dry-cleaned. When Owen and

I returned to our room about an hour and a half later, it was there waiting for us. Very impressive, we thought. And it had been worth the brief inconvenience just to see my husband drenched in eggs and hollandaise sauce! It was a sight to behold and brought all of us a lot of laughs.

Every week I flew over to the Bradenton factory in a small two-seater plane. It was just the pilot and me. He was the same guy who sold me the ticket, carried my briefcase, and flew the plane. In the summertime, the thunder and lightning storms were so fierce that the plane tilted forward, backward, and sideways. I'll never know how I was brave enough to do this. It was probably because I *had* to.

DONZI DASH

In 1987, Roscioli International elevated the fleet of sportfishing yachts to another level. Bob Roscioli went on to build four or five different models after that and has built more than seventy-five yachts over the past thirty years.

The Donzi by Roscioli trademark stood for "classic, fluid lines, rugged 'go anywhere' seaworthiness, impressive nimbleness, and the ultimate in finishes and interior appointments." I know I sound as if I am PR-ing you, but this was (and is) the truth.

To demonstrate the Donzi brand's fitness, we brainstormed and conceived the idea of the Donzi Dash. It would take place in 1988, with the goal of setting a record time going from Florida to Puerto Rico, thus proving the merits of the Roscioli-built Donzi Z-65 convertible. It was easier to come here than to go the other way, so Bob wanted to reverse directions in order to set a record.

I was able to convince the bible of the boating industry, *Motor Boating & Sailing,* to send its senior editor John Clemans along to document the journey. In addition, to mark the end of the Donzi Dash run, we were planning a large press event in Puerto Rico so that the media coverage would extend beyond John's article. We were certain that this type of marketing would help sell the Roscioli's new Donzi Z-65 model.

Richie Koch of New York, owner of the six-month-old *Libra II* (one of Roscioli's new Donzi Z-65s), was kind enough to let us use his yacht in the

Donzi Dash. Richie planned to compete in the Thirty-Fifth Annual Club Nautico International Billfish Tournament, which would take place in San Juan.

"Captain John" (professional Captain John Huard) frequently worked for Roscioli, and this time was no exception. He flew to New York and then ran the vessel down to Fort Lauderdale along with Koch's full-time captain, Eddie Ferret, in a record time of two days. For the trek to San Juan, that Donzi Z-65 would also carry journalist John Clemans and a photographer from *Motor Boating & Sailing*; Steve Jones, Roscioli's warranty manager; John Murray, Don Gollot, and Todd Layman (three technicians from Stewart & Stevenson) to watch over the craft's powerful diesel engines; and another seasoned captain, Captain Pedro Panzcardi, who would be making his two hundredth trip from Florida to Puerto Rico.

Walter Fournier, a Puerto Rican businessman who wanted a Donzi yacht dealership in the Caribbean, was so happy about the event that he lent his Cessna Citation II jet and pilot for the trip. Fournier knew that this would be a big promotion for Donzi in Puerto Rico and that it would benefit him if he became a dealer. His plane had scouted the fuel stops the previous week. Fuel trucks and customs agents were on alert. Everything was ready to go.

The challenge was to make the one-thousand-statute-mile run from Fort Lauderdale to San Juan in thirty-six hours with fuel stops in San Salvador and South Caicos. Extra fuel was housed in large rubber "bladder" tanks that took up a lot of room on the boat. Borrowed from publishing executive Steve Forbes, those bladder tanks looked like beached whales! The loan occurred because John Huard, Bob Roscioli's captain, knew Forbes's captain.

I planned to fly to San Juan for our press event. Owen would be waiting for me there because he was arriving a day or two early to get some R and R, which included a bit of gambling. I hoped he would still have his shirt on when I got there.

The *Libra II* departed from SE Seventeenth Street in Fort Lauderdale on a Wednesday night, nearly two hours late, in rain and lightning. Captain Pedro didn't come along after all. He didn't like the looks of the weather. As the yacht was pulling away that night, I was standing on the dock, watching and worrying. I was concerned about the weather conditions and the extra fuel aboard.

John Clemans thought that he shouldn't have come along either when, later that night, the motion of the Atlantic Ocean became so forceful that he fell from his bunk. According to John's documentation, the vessel was "crashing through the night. Great walls of water flew by on both sides. The boat seemed airborne most of the time, slamming back down with a loud jarring crack and a shudder that made even Huard wince; but not only was he 'not stopping'—he wasn't slowing down either. Our whole game plan—the waiting fuel trucks, the obliging customs agents, the Friday victory bash at Club Nautico, the record itself—was based on maintaining at least thirty knots, and Huard wasn't about to give up just three hours into the trip."

The turbulence resulted in a minor loss. A glass shelf in the refrigerator had slivered into pieces, and much of the fried chicken and fruit salad they were planning to eat spilled onto the floor when the refrigerator door was opened. "The Donzi Dash was fast turning into the Donzi Diet," John wrote. "But losing food was of little consequence because eating in such circumstances was out of the question."

It was a rough ride but the Donzi Z-65 continued through the darkness. By sunrise the waves were eight-to-ten footers. The vessel was two hours behind the anticipated running time and four hours behind schedule. In addition, a slight exhaust leak had developed during the night causing smoke to spew out the back of the boat. The air filters were filling up every few hours as well.

Nevertheless, the *Libra II* pulled into a marina in San Salvador in the Bahamas on Thursday at around 1:30 p.m. instead of the scheduled 8:00 a.m. Although the fuel trucks were waiting, it was too late to head for South Caicos, one of the islands in the Turks and Caicos archipelago. They wouldn't make it before dark, and there were risky reefs in the area. So everyone aboard headed over to the Riding Rock Inn, cleaned up, ate, and slept in a comfortable bed that evening. By then, the record run concept was at risk. They had selected the most direct route possible—straight across the Bahamas and then straight down to Puerto Rico—not how it is typically done. There also were three low-pressure systems in the Caribbean that week, each interacting with the other. The seas were not favorable for being on the open ocean. Everyone knew it was a gamble even before they had set out for this voyage.

The boat left San Salvador before sunrise on Friday so that it would reach South Caicos, a two-hundred-and-fifty-mile run, before nightfall.

"As soon as we turned southeast around the tip of San Salvador, the ocean smacked us right in the face," John wrote. "When we stopped to switch from the bladder tanks to the main tanks, the horizon tilted back and forth like a seesaw as waves washed by, level with the bridge. The odds of reaching South Caicos by dark were getting longer by the minute, which presented the first serious threat of the trip. We continued to slog it out as squalls rushed at us out of the east."

Taking a new course that was ninety degrees off the original course was somewhat advantageous. In spite of the rough ride, the harbor at South Caicos was almost in sight; it was around 7:00 p.m. on Friday. As the captain made the turn to enter the inlet, the starboard propeller clipped a reef and was down. This caused an emergency that had to be repaired before they could proceed.

John Clemans's words captured it all. "BANG! We hit. *Libra II* shuddered violently as Huard leapt for the throttles. We were able to keep going but only at idle speed. Suddenly it was dark. We inched into the entrance to the South Caicos harbor guided by lights. A stiff breeze blew straight in, which made docking a crippled boat a touch-and-go exercise. A group of people stood along the sea wall where we tied up. There was no marina. Behind them was a fuel truck. Huard was crushed. To have come this far under such adverse conditions in so short a time was a remarkable achievement, and had we been able to push on, we might have set a time that would be hard to beat in *calm* seas. Now, however, we found ourselves in contention for a far different sort of record: longest stay on South Caicos."

When I heard that the *Libra II* was marooned in South Caicos, and knowing that John Clemans was aboard, I wanted to be there. So I flew there in a small prop airplane with Tom Glass from Roscioli. But I was not happy about it. Unbeknown to me, we were traveling to an area that was like a

Third-World country. The runway had bumps and potholes. Trained dogs chased the wild boars, donkeys, goats, and other creatures away just before we landed. And we had to land during daylight hours because there were no lights on the runway.

Then we saw dusty roads, sheds, shacks, and even more creepy animals. One of the primitive shacks served as the forsaken airport. I remember looking out the window from that airport and seeing roaches so big, I could have put saddles on them! I also noticed that the ground outside was covered with broken pieces of green glass. Someone told me that drug runners came to the island to hide. They apparently drank St. Pauli Girl beer in green bottles and then became rowdy. I couldn't blame them. Who *wouldn't* want to drink in this place, which looked abandoned and in such sad shape?

In the meantime, my loving husband was having fun in San Juan. It wasn't fair. Not fair at all. But I knew that life wasn't always fair. I carried on.

When Tom and I asked about accommodations for an overnight stay, we were directed to the French whorehouse. I couldn't believe it! That was a place I did *not* want to be. But there was no other choice. The whorehouse turned out to be the Admiral Arms Hotel, which reminded us of a rundown Old Florida-style single-story motel. It was shut down, but we convinced the proprietor to open up for us and everyone aboard the *Libra II*. He gave us several rooms and fed us. I knew I wouldn't sleep a wink that night because I didn't feel safe. I also saw rats and some other animals I had never seen before! The good news, however, was that the proprietor of this "establishment" was able to call the Roscioli facility in Fort Lauderdale to tell them that the yacht was stranded.

Early the next morning, a dive into the water by Steve Jones revealed that the shafts, struts, and rudders were okay, but there was a mangled propeller on the starboard side. There were no facilities on the island to deal with this problem. John Clemans was preparing to fly back to Florida in three days, since that was the earliest flight out. From there, he would return to his office in New York. But, fortunately, John had miscalculated both the resources and resourcefulness of the Roscioli Yachting Center.

Roscioli's prop man, Rui Conde, had worked on a spare propeller through the night in Fort Lauderdale, just in case that turned out to be the problem. Since it was, Tom and I flew to Fort Lauderdale the next morning aboard the Cessna with its pilot. He removed the rear seats of the plane so that the substitute prop, prop puller, wrenches, and diving gear could be placed inside. The three of us and our cargo were back in South Caicos by 3:30 p.m., and Steve and Eddie then reinstalled the propeller.

The boat left South Caicos early that Saturday evening. About a mile out, smoke was detected, which was just a short, probably from a wire that had come loose somewhere. The problem was quickly remedied.

Although the course was again altered, the ocean remained merciless. Clogged fuel filters and an air leak in the cockpit tank caused the boat to lose power a few times, but this glitch was rectified by the technicians who were on board.

An hour before sunrise on Sunday morning, they were seventy-five miles from Puerto Rico's western tip, about to enter the Mona Passage, which was considered to be the roughest section of the entire route.

"By now, however, blasting along through the darkness on a bucking one-hundred-thousand-pound boat seemed an eminently reasonable thing to be doing," John continued to write. They were in the home stretch. "After forty hours of lurching through life, the prospect of level ground had all the appeal of stale beer. Indeed, despite the groans, the bruises and the 'never agains,' the grueling rhythm of the run had become a way of life, an almost sensual experience."

The *Libra II* was met in San Juan by three escort vessels, and helicopters hovering overhead. "We felt like heroes home from war. We passed El Moro at the entrance to the San Juan Harbor exactly forty-seven running hours after leaving Fort Lauderdale. We had hoped to do it in thirty-six hours, and had the seas been calm, we could have."

They failed to set a record as far as time, but the Donzi Dash proved to be more than a long rough run in a large sportfisherman. According to the senior editor of *Motor Boating & Sailing*, it was "the ultimate sea trial—a far greater test of the magnificent Donzi than any calm-water marathon could ever be…Donzi 65s are 'overbuilt' for just such offshore mayhem as we encountered…I doubt that any other production sportfisherman of any size could have equaled the Donzi's performance. The boat's combination of speed and strength was remarkable."

I should have kissed John Clemans for his rave review.

Tom and I had flown from South Caicos to San Juan and were waiting for the *Libra II* when it arrived. We were delighted to discover that the only thing on the inside that had broken was the refrigerator shelf. There were no cracked mirrors, no water leakage, and the engines hadn't budged on their beds. Furthermore, six thousand pounds of bagged fuel had moved around the cockpit, pushing against the transom from the inside, yet the transom door was still perfectly aligned.

After I had landed in San Juan earlier that day, I checked into the beautiful, clean room at the Caribe Hilton where Owen was already staying. I immediately shed my clothes and showered. I was absolutely schmutzig! As I was standing and lathering myself, I watched the thick dust and mud pour off my body. Not only did it make a huge dark ring around the white surface of the tub, but it looked like I had dumped a wheelbarrow full of dirt in the middle. I then changed clothes and felt like a new woman.

I reflect back now on my courage. There were no mobile phones, no Internet connections, and no MapQuest during those years. I had been in South Caicos and went wherever I needed to be. I was committed to doing anything that had to be done for a client.

There was a great turnout for our press event at Club Nautico, and the Donzi Dash had validated the speed and seaworthiness of the Donzi Z-65. This powerful machine was touted as one of the fastest and largest sportfishermans in the world. That was good news for anyone who loved to fish. What a fisherman cares most about is how fast he can get into the deep water and cast a line.

This was wonderful news for the Rosciolis too.

John Clemans's nine-page *Motor Boating & Sailing* feature article entitled "1,000 Miles of Rough Water" still hangs on the wall in the Roscioli office today. It was published in November 1988.

Even though I heard that Captain John had proclaimed "No more boat trips" while he was having dinner in Old San Juan, he later took Roscioli's new Donzi Z-65 from Fort Lauderdale to the Atlantic City Boat Show.

I guess getting back onto a boat is like getting back onto a horse.

WHEN PR ISN'T PUBLIC RELATIONS

While Bob Roscioli was negotiating with the Puerto Rican entrepreneur Walter Fournier about giving him the right to a Donzi dealership in the Caribbean, Bob found out there was a federal law stating that if you allow someone to represent you, then they have that right forever. Bob didn't want to extend that right infinitely. For one thing, Fournier represented other boat companies such as Bertram. For another, Bob had only gotten his Donzi dealership a year before and he didn't know what the future would bring. So when it got down to the nitty gritty, Bob didn't want to be locked in. He squashed the deal. Consequently, Fournier became bitter and sued Bob's company even though they had never signed a deal.

Of course, I agreed to be deposed after Bob had asked me to. The deposition was held in Miami. I was joined by Bob, his attorney, Fournier's attorney (who spoke only broken English), and the court stenographer. As I was being questioned, my responses continued to upset Fournier's attorney. He became a lunatic, slamming his fists on the table and then waving his arms in the air. I was clueless as to why he reacted in such an agitated manner.

As it turned out, most of my responses were about my company handling Roscioli's PR. Whenever I uttered "PR," which occurred frequently during the deposition, he thought I meant Puerto Ricans, and that I was debasing and being disrespectful to the Puerto Rican people!

TREASURE CAY

Soon after Donzi by Roscioli International introduced its Donzi Z-65, I was also able to secure a cover story in a South Florida–based boating publication.

The editor wanted to put a photograph of several of those new vessels on the front cover. So we set up a photo shoot.

I arranged with Bob Roscioli to bring four Donzi Z-65s to Treasure Cay in the Bahamas, where the shoot would take place. We wanted to line up the yachts in a semicircular configuration. This took a lot of maneuvering, and I was tasked with jumping from the bow of one boat onto each of the others to give the respective captains their instructions. I was nimble and in good shape, so this shouldn't have been a challenge. But for *me* it was an escapade because I didn't know how to swim! I was absolutely terrified. I'm admitting this now, although I've never admitted this to anyone, including my children and grandchildren.

ATLANTIC CITY BOAT SHOW

The Rosciolis displayed their yachts at many of the nation's boat shows. They'd go to shows in Norfolk, Annapolis, Atlantic City, and Fort Lauderdale, to name a few of the locations. The boats in Atlantic City were docked at the Farley State Marina. It was located across from the Trump Castle Hotel Casino, where we stayed whenever Owen and I attended that show.

During one of the Atlantic City shows, I reached out to ABC's *Good Morning America*. The Miss America Pageant was taking place at the same time, so I arranged to have some of the beauty contestants interviewed aboard a Donzi Z-65 during their broadcast. Apart from that, we also invited all of the contestants onto the vessel and took a photograph of them.

That was a very memorable trip for us for other reasons as well. Bob Roscioli had a prospective customer, Bob McMurtrie, who was in the real estate and banking businesses. *My* Bob anticipated that the other Bob (McMurtrie) would be purchasing a new yacht from him during this boat show. McMurtrie's current yacht was moored at the Farley State Marina too. Because McMurtrie was a high roller known to Trump Castle's management for winning a lot of money and losing a lot of money, they "comped" the large suite that Bob Roscioli had reserved for him. I remember that we filled the bathtub with ice to keep bottles of fine champagne cold for him.

Being a player on a grand scale, McMurtrie had a lot of clout at the casino, and his yacht captain Tommy Fox was a take-charge kind of guy. For instance, if they walked into a restaurant at Trump Castle and McMurtrie pointed out a table he wanted, even if it was occupied, Fox would tell the maître d' to move the people elsewhere so that he and McMurtrie could sit there. The request would be met.

On that first night, Bob Roscioli went in the casino with McMurtrie and Tommy Fox, who also served as McMurtrie's bodyguard. They sat at a private table. Lady Luck was on McMurtrie's side. He won well over a million dollars as he gambled and drank the night away. Instead of getting a cashier's check in the amount of his winnings, he asked for cash. Fox took the cash and wrapped it in a tablecloth, then carried it over his shoulder onto McMurtrie's yacht and hid it underneath McMurtrie's bed.

The next day Bob Roscioli woke up early because he had another client at the boat show: Jim Orthwein, who was part of the Busch family and the largest stockholder in Budweiser. In order to outdo Orthwein, McMurtrie invited Bob, Tommy, Orthwein, and his boat captain onto his sixty-foot ocean sportfisherman. Wanting to demonstrate the influence he had at Trump Castle, McMurtrie arranged for four servers from the hotel to board his yacht with trays of hors d'oeuvres and buckets filled with bottles of Cristal and Dom Pérignon champagnes, estimated at about $500 a pop. McMurtrie, a real jokester, asked Orthwein if he had ever had a champagne fight. After Orthwein said he had not, McMurtrie said, "Let me show you how it's done, Jim." McMurtrie proceeded to uncork a bottle of Dom Pérignon and spray its contents all over Orthwein. In turn, Orthwein grabbed a bottle and did the same thing to McMurtrie.

Not wanting all of the champagne to go to waste, Bob Roscioli told his own captain to grab two of the sealed bottles and take them to his yacht, where they would enjoy them. But this never happened. McMurtrie pushed Bob's captain, who was carrying those pricey bottles, into the water!

This is how "boys will be boys" with their toys.

After getting cleaned up, McMurtrie, Bob Roscioli, and Tommy Fox were back in the casino. In a matter of about twenty minutes, McMurtrie lost

$750,000. Consequently, my client Bob lost out on the sale of a new yacht to McMurtrie.

We also met Ivana Trump on that trip to Atlantic City. She was still married to Donald at the time, and her yacht was docked at the Farley State Marina. I don't recall exactly how we were introduced, but she graciously invited Bob Roscioli, Owen, and me aboard for a cruise and cocktail reception, which we thoroughly enjoyed. Ivana was just as charming as she was beautiful.

MONKEY BUSINESS

When Bob Roscioli sold real estate developer Jeffrey Soffer of Turnberry Associates a yacht during the nineties, Jeffrey called the new yacht *Monkey Business*. But it wasn't the *infamous Monkey Business* that had been custom designed for Turnberry Isle Resort in Aventura and purchased by his father Don Soffer years before. *That* eighty-three-foot Broward yacht became associated with ruining Gary Hart's political career. Hart, a former US Senator from Colorado, chartered the (first) *Monkey Business* and went to Bimini in 1987, prior to announcing his campaign for US president. Hart was widely perceived as a front-runner for the Democratic nomination in 1988. But someone had taken a photograph of a young blonde, Donna Rice, sitting on Hart's lap aboard the yacht, and it surfaced in the media. The photo confirmed Hart's suspected affair with Rice and resulted in a huge scandal, which quashed his hopes of a presidential run.

Was it really surprising that this philanderer was aboard a yacht named *Monkey Business?*

ROSCIOLI GOLF CLASSICS

During the time we represented the Rosciolis, Bob was asked to help raise funds for Our Lady Queen of Martyrs School in Fort Lauderdale. His daughter was an eighth grader at the school, and his son had graduated two years earlier and was attending St. Thomas Aquinas. The middle school had never had air conditioning, and it was badly needed.

Bob didn't want to do something that would raise nickels and dimes. He wanted to raise *real* money by doing something in a big way. He told me that the community had been good to him, and he wanted to give back by working hard for the cause.

With my help and the Rosciolis' connections, we launched the First Annual Roscioli Classic Celebrity Golf Tournament at Bonaventure Resort & Spa in 1987. The two-day event included a cocktail party, auction, entertainment, and a "Meet the Stars" preview on Thursday night. On Friday, there was a golf clinic prior to the shot-gun start. That evening, there was another cocktail party, as well as dinner and a show with live performances. Bert Parks was the emcee. The event attracted more than three hundred fifty golfers and celebrities such as football great Joe Namath, singers Bobby Rydell and Don Cornell, actor Jeff MacKay (a regular on *Magnum, P.I.*), country music songwriter Dave Loggins, and comedian Freddie Roman. George Barrie, the former owner of Faberge Cosmetics, brought a ten-piece orchestra from New York City to perform. The event was like a Hollywood premiere.

George Barrie was an accomplished musician, songwriter, and film producer. He also was one of the first people to have celebrities endorse a product. George had created Brut cologne for men and made Joe Namath the spokesperson. The Rosciolis had sold George a yacht, so we got to know him personally, and we all socialized together from time to time. We had a ball!

R. Moulder Jr., the principal from Our Lady Queen of Martyrs School, was thrilled with the amount of money raised from the event, since it would pay for the school's air conditioning. She told a writer from the *Miami Herald's Neighbors* section that "It would have taken ten years of candy sales and raffles to do this."

Bob had nothing to gain from his efforts. At most, his daughter, Heather, would enjoy a month or two of air conditioning before she graduated. Still, Bob was committed to a quality Catholic education and wanted to help other kids.

Riding on the waves of that event's success, the Second Annual Roscioli Classic Celebrity Golf Tournament followed at Bonaventure. The proceeds from this event, which also attracted hundreds of golfers, were used to purchase computers for the kids at the school. Don Cornell, jazz and pop vocalist Sylvia Bennett, and comedian and actor "Woody" Woodbury were among the celebrities who participated. Funds far exceeded those raised in the first event.

For the Rosciolis' third annual event, proceeds went to the Roscioli Foundation for Education to benefit private and parochial schools in Broward County. Regretfully, that was the last time a Roscioli Classic was held because of the many months of preplanning required. It simply became too time consuming, and Bob and Sharon had a business to run.

The Adler Network represented the Rosciolis for about eight or nine years, and these were only a few examples of their generosity. I've stayed in touch with Bob and Sharon, and we still enjoy reminiscing. When we bring up all these memories, it feels just like yesterday. And I will be forever thankful that they added the dimension of yachting to my life, even though I still do *not* know how to swim.

CHAPTER 7

Ar+Vi+Da

I DOUBT THAT BOCA RATON would have turned out to be the world-class city that it is today had it not been for a forward-thinking land speculator named Arthur Vining Davis. Thanks to his vision and extensive land holdings, which he purchased back in the fifties, Boca slowly morphed from a small sleepy farming village into an alluring internationally recognized community.

A bit of a history lesson is on order to explain how and why this occurred.

Davis is said to have owned more than one hundred thousand acres in Florida alone, as well as land in Cuba and the Bahamas. Considering that he reportedly paid only a few hundred dollars per acre, he would one day become a very wealthy man.

He introduced the "sport of kings," polo, to Boca Raton in 1955. A year later, he purchased and began managing the Boca Raton Resort and Club, the historic property built in the 1926. At that time, it was called the Ritz-Carlton Cloister Inn.

A former chairman of Alcoa, Davis used the one hundred thousand acres that he had amassed as assets and transferred them into a new public corporation, the Arvida Corporation, in 1958. The company utilized the first two letters of Davis's full name: Ar + Vi + Da. An astute businessman, he retained sixty percent of the stock for himself. Stock sales provided capital to develop the Royal Palm Yacht and Country Club on the Intracoastal Waterway in Boca Raton, which replaced the polo fields. He relocated those fields west on Glades Road.

When Arvida went public, Davis became chairman of the board but had little to do with its daily operations. Pompano Beach real estate broker and banker, Milton Weir, became the company's first president. He remained until 1960. Following the selection of an interim successor, Stockton, Whatley, Davin and Company of Jacksonville, Florida, was then hired to manage Arvida. Brown L. Whatley was named president and CEO of Arvida in 1961.

Although Davis died in 1962, his legacy continued with the development of much of Boca Raton and the southwestern communities of Palm Beach County. There was development in Miami-Dade and Broward counties too. Arvida perpetuated Davis's desire for Arvida communities to carry out the tradition of elegance that reflected his own carefree way of life.

Upon Davis's death, a group of banks took over Arvida's majority ownership while leaving the company's management to Whatley. In those early years, Arvida was primarily a land bank rather than a development firm. Profits were derived from the sale of its land. In 1965, the controlling stock was sold to the Pennsylvania Railroad, which then merged with the New York Central Railroad to become Penn Central.

In 1969, Arvida added the landmark "Pink Tower" to the Boca Raton Resort and Club. Soaring twenty-seven-stories high, it remained the tallest building in Palm Beach County for many years. In 1970, even though Penn Central declared bankruptcy and reorganized, Arvida prospered. In 1971, Pennco (the real estate subsidiary of Penn Central with a controlling interest in Arvida) ended Whatley's management contract and hired California developer Charles Cobb. Cobb became Arvida's chairman of the board and is said to have infused new life into the company.

In 1973, Richard Miller was hired to manage Arvida's major Boca Raton residential and commercial developments, which included Boca West Country Club, the Arvida Park of Commerce near the IBM campus (where the original IBM personal computer was designed and manufactured), the Boca Raton Resort and Club, and several western area communities. During the recession of 1973–75, Arvida was able to endure because it had very little under construction at the time.

John Temple joined Arvida in 1975 and, in just seven years, became the president of its resort communities and real estate companies. Previously held publicly, the company's stock became privately owned in 1976.

Arvida built the Boca Raton Resort and Club's Boca Beach Club fronting the ocean, which opened in 1980. The Town Center Mall, developed by Arvida and JMB/Federated Realty, was completed that same year. In 1983, Arvida was sold to a group of Arvida executives, including John Temple. He remained at the helm during Boca's real estate boom period of the eighties. After the Disney Corporation took over Arvida in 1984, John stayed on. When Disney sold Arvida, John left and began his own development firm in 1987.

As you can see, Arvida underwent many changes throughout the years. In spite of this—or because of this—the company helped change the face of the city of Boca Raton and some of its unincorporated areas. It moved forward into areas never before considered for development.

WESTWARD HO

The arrival of Florida's Turnpike (then called the Sunshine State Parkway), followed by I-95 into southern Palm Beach County, initiated a westward movement in both residential and commercial properties. During the seventies, Arvida created the residential communities of Estancia, Millpond, Paseos, and Timbercreek.

As early as 1971, Arvida began plans for a 1,436-acre parcel of land that the Adler Network would eventually become involved in: *Boca West.* The land was still mostly agricultural, but with most of the construction taking place between 1973 and 1988, it was transformed into Arvida's flagship residential resort community. Located on the north side of Glades Road between the turnpike to the west and Jog Road to the east, Boca West became the only master-planned community in the area at that time to offer equity membership in four championship golf courses, more than thirty tennis courts, an aquatic center with three swimming pools, and a new, multilevel, multifunction club center, all within its gates. Boca West also was pleasing to the eye because it reflected thoughtful development with a wide choice of townhomes, patio homes, villas, condo apartments, and single-family homes situated within fifty four residential villages.

Today this location is considered to be centralized. During the seventies, however, most people (other than the Arvida team) thought it was in the middle of the Everglades! There were alligators, land crabs, and God knows what other creatures prowling around! Who would possibly want to live or vacation *that* far west, even if the private villages within Boca West bordered lush golf course landscapes, wooded areas, and waterways? Even if there were residences offered at varying price points and buyers could socialize and play where they lived?

The answer was approximately 3,380 families, or six thousand residents. Arvida was right on the money.

The Adler Network first became involved at Boca West when we were hired to represent three of the builders there: Hank Yusem, Sol Slossberg, and Dick Siemans. (Siemans would later become the driving force behind the Polo Club of Boca Raton, Gleneagles Country Club in Delray Beach, the Delray Medical Center, and West Boca Medical Center. He retained our public relations firm to help market the Polo Club.)

We had produced brochures for those three builders, and Arvida was very impressed with them. Arvida then hired us to produce a brochure to promote the entire community of Boca West.

The success of Boca West, in large measure, was due to the migration from the Northeast Corridor of empty nesters, pre-retirees and retirees. As an example, many residents of Levittown in the town of Hempstead on Long Island had purchased their small homes in 1947 for as little as $6,990, with little money down. Levittown, the first mass-produced suburb in the United States, was built between 1947 and 1951 by Levitt & Sons. Using assembly-line methodology, the boxlike homes were affordable for middle-class families headed by white and blue collar workers and became the foundation for the "master-planned community" of the future. Although these residences had a cookie-cutter appearance, this became less evident due to curving streets and landscaping, as well as exterior home maintenance guidelines.

During the seventies and eighties, homes like those in Levittown had appreciated substantially in value. Therefore, many people from New York sold their homes for a big profit and relocated to Boca West as permanent residents. Or they retained their homes up north and bought vacation homes in Boca West with the intention of becoming permanent residents later on. Until then, they became snowbirds. This was a dream come true for these buyers. A fantasy they could *live*. They escaped the frigid north during the winter months and instead were surrounded by palm trees, golf courses, water features, white herons, and egrets. They resided in paradise and enjoyed all of the resort trappings offered to them. This movement became quite a phenomenon, and Boca West was ideally positioned to play into it.

We too were blessed to have witnessed it *and* been a part of it. We also were well suited to help Boca West sustain its sales momentum.

As was the case with many other country club communities that followed, Boca West began with wilderness that underwent a metamorphosis. Sales associates at its various village sales centers sold residences by showing only a master site plan, map, residential product renderings, and floor plans. Sometimes there were furnished models to help buyers better visualize their purchases. Either way, they bought because there was a home for every taste and wallet, and each village had its own character. They were lured by the thought of living an active, carefree life in a subtropical paradise. No one could blame them. And others envied them.

At Boca West, we worked closely with Fred DeFalco, a proven real estate sales leader. After serving as vice president with Coldwell Banker in Baltimore, he relocated to Clearwater, Florida, to run its Florida west coast division. In 1989, Fred founded a real estate consulting company, and the Arvida Corporation became a client of his in Boca Raton. When the consulting contract ended, Arvida recruited him. He became the executive vice president and broker who operated Arvida Realty Sales, an Arvida subsidiary.

Premier Club Memberships
Even if you have heard about Premier Club membership at the Boca Raton Resort and Club, you may not know that this membership program was initially conceived to serve Boca West residents.

The powers that be at the resort realized that many of the residents at the western country club community wanted access to the beach. The Boca Beach Club could easily satisfy that desire. So every owner at Boca West was given a free Premier Club membership during their first year. While that free membership provided yet another incentive to purchase at Boca West, the Premier Club sales team hoped to convert many of those free memberships into paid memberships the following year at a cost of $5,000 each. This would become a cash cow for the resort, providing a steady stream of additional income.

The resort retained the Adler Network to help. That's when I first met Dan Wielhouwer. Dan's forte was creating and implementing imaginative marketing strategies and campaigns for high-end country clubs, resorts, and yacht clubs. He was vice president of club sales and marketing at the resort. His assistant was Candace Jorritsma (who years later became an independent real estate marketing consultant). And Dan's wife Deanna was the secretary for John Temple, Arvida's president. It was a very tightly knit group.

Dan was very smart, but he wouldn't prepare for meetings until the eleventh hour. Candace tried to keep him organized. Nevertheless, we'd have to gather around the copy machine at the last minute to produce the materials needed for the Premier Club meetings. Somehow we got things done in the nick of time.

That is also when I met Michael Glennie, president of the Boca Raton Resort and Club. He had previously been the general manager of the Waldorf Astoria in Manhattan. Michael knew a great deal about the hospitality industry. He was world-wise, very gallant, and had a polished presence. I was particularly in awe every time I saw him walk around the resort. He seemed to know every employee. He was friendly and kind to each one of them, whether they were part of the housekeeping, concierge, or food and beverage staffs.

This was an example of exceptionally good internal *public relations.*

Michael must have liked me because whenever I called, his secretary said he'd be happy to speak with me. Apparently, it wasn't always easy to get through to him on the first try.

To engage Boca West residents, we helped the Premier Club create an Ambassador's Club, with appointed "ambassadors" from each residential village. Those ambassadors were given red jackets and pins with the resort's emblem to wear. They invited their neighbors to meetings and cocktail receptions where they'd learn about the benefits of a membership at the resort and meet some of the resort managers. This worked like a well-oiled machine. Dan Wielhouwer and Michael Glennie spoke, and then they introduced the audience to the head chef, the banquet services manager, and others. These events were held either in the Pink Tower or in the resort proper. Each one was first class and very well orchestrated. Prospective Premier Club members were, quite simply, wined, dined, and dazzled. All of these efforts paid off because the Boca West program was a success. Many residents of that community became members of the resort—and gladly *paid* for the privilege.

It then made a lot of sense for a world-class resort, with a beautiful beach club and other affiliated properties, to reach beyond Boca West with its exclusive Premier Club membership concept. Therefore, after our efforts were finished at Boca West, the Boca Raton Resort and Club retained our agency to expand the target market.

A Premier Club membership became an enviable one to have. It was transferable to the children of a member or to the buyer of a member's residence in either Palm Beach or Broward counties. However, residency or property ownership was not a requirement. There were various membership packages, with a membership fee and dues, available. Members would also pay daily-use fees for a spa treatment, dining, use of a beach cabana, a round of golf, and so forth.

The Adler Network studied the history of the Boca Raton Resort and Club, which dated back to its opening in 1926, and then wrote articles about it. There was a very colorful history to tell, including how architect and developer Addison Mizner had walked around the resort in pajamas or a robe with his monkey, Johnnie Brown, perched on his shoulder. That exotic pet is still buried in Via Mizner, a courtyard off Worth Avenue in Palm Beach. Mizner sometimes had a parrot on his shoulder too.

Or, if an original ceramic or porcelain tile at the resort had to be replaced, the resort would go to great lengths to obtain a replacement from the original source. We'd interview that source, and because there was an interesting story to relate, we disseminated it to the media. There were a lot of other things to convey about the resort's rich historical heritage as well.

We became very involved in real estate broker community outreach as it related to the Premier Club's Membership Referral and Incentive Program for Palm Beach County Realtors. There were hundreds of real estate professionals who could provide a qualified base of potential club members to the Premier Club's sales and marketing team. So we held annual broker breakfasts and later annual broker cocktail receptions, which became big events with over a thousand real estate professionals in attendance. For them, the resort was the place to "be seen." Awards were given out for referrals or to the Realtors with the most referrals as a way for the resort to show its appreciation. But it was a two-way street, making it a win-win for Realtors too. The option of being able to enjoy the pleasures and pastimes inherent in a Premier Club membership helped those brokers and realtors market and sell homes, especially those located in "unamenitized" neighborhoods.

Arvida Revisited

Today Boca West remains one of the country's largest private equity-owned clubs. Furthermore, the Arvida name lived on long after Boca West was completed and matured into one of its most prized communities.

I always admired Arvida's core value. It wasn't only to sell real estate. The company set out and succeeded in creating communities that were pleasurable and aesthetically pleasing for their residents. It provided parklike settings, lush landscaping, open spaces, and water features, not to mention an array of recreational, sports, and social amenities and hospitality services.

I especially liked that Arvida used its name on signage at Boca West and its other communities. This enhanced the company's brand recognition. Throughout our years in business, we always suggested to our other developer clients that they include their corporate name as a tagline following the name of their new communities and on on-site signage.

Arvida went on to develop high-end condominiums in Boca Raton such as the Addison and Presidential Place. The development company is further credited with creating other upscale, planned, residential communities with resort amenities, including Broken Sound and Weston. All told, since Arthur Vining Davis founded his company in 1958, Arvida developed more than sixty planned communities with more than forty thousand new homes and thirty golf courses in Florida, Georgia, South Carolina, North Carolina, Texas, and California.

After Arvida was sold several more times, in 1997 the St. Joe Company acquired its assets, and Arvida became the community development arm of the St. Joe Company. In 2004, Arvida underwent a name change to St. Joe Towns & Resorts.

Before concluding this chapter, I want to point out that *today's* country club is no longer the country club of our parents or grandparents. Younger residents are moving in to replace an aging population, and community amenities and services are changing to serve a more youthful demographic. This is injecting new life into them, keeping them financially solvent, and preserving them for generations to come.

CHAPTER 8

Sophia

ITALIAN-BORN FILM AND TELEVISION ACTRESS Sophia Loren lent her name and elegant European tastes as a creative consultant to the Trump Group (*no relation to Donald Trump*) when their master-planned waterfront community of Williams Island in Aventura, Florida, was in its early stage of development. Jules Trump, his wife Stephanie, and brother Eddie envisioned the exclusive community as the "Florida Riviera," and they thought that Sophia would be the perfect person to help them create an environment that emulated the Italian Riviera in many ways. They were absolutely right.

Before the Trumps contacted the screen icon and sought her advice about their project, they asked me what I thought of the idea. This was in the early to mid eighties when I was representing interior designer Ted Fine of Fine Decorators. Ted had been commissioned to create the interiors of many of the new model residences at Williams Island as well as the condo buildings' public spaces. That's how I knew the Trump family. In addition, Ted would later be hired by numerous Williams Island residents (particularly those originating from the Northeast Corridor) to design their interiors.

Sophia Loren was one of the most beloved figures in the international film world. She had won an Academy Award for Best Actress in a foreign-language film (*Two Women*) in 1962, as well as several Golden Globes. She was married to the love of *her* life, producer Carlo Ponti, and together they had two young sons. Aside from her talent, she was a timeless beauty. She was sophisticated and had traveled the world. I believed that Sophia had everything in her favor and that her input would be very helpful in shaping the image of Williams Island. After I communicated my opinion to the Trumps, they reached out to her. They might have done so even if I hadn't given them *my* Good Housekeeping Seal of Approval!

Jules, Stephanie, and Eddie have said that they designed Williams Island to imitate the charming Mediterranean village of Procida, one of the Phlegraean Islands off the coast of Naples in southern Italy. (Similar to Portofino, Procida is a village on the Italian Riviera coastline thought to have a bit more character.) While consulting with Sophia, the Trumps accompanied her to Procida because she wanted to show it to them first hand. Consequently, the new Florida community blended the scenic sophistication of the Italian Riviera with the state's natural resources.

The Trump family also encouraged Sophia to become a resident of Williams Island. She had several homes elsewhere, so why not have one in South Florida as well? After discussing this idea with her husband Carlo, they moved ahead with the suggestion. They also commissioned Ted Fine to create the interiors of their new residence. After Ted had finished, I met and spent several days with the film star. Those days were among the most enjoyable days of my professional life.

I had arranged for South Florida photographer Dan Forer to professionally photograph the interiors of Sophia's condominium for Ted. Then I reached out to Paige Rense, the editor of the esteemed *Architectural Digest*. She was interested in seeing the pictures and liked what she saw after I sent them to her. Dan was frequently contracted by that magazine to shoot for them, so that was another plus in our favor. Then, with Sophia's permission, the magazine would interview her, and Dan would take photos of her.

An early riser, Sophia was waiting for me when I arrived at her residence on the first morning of her photo shoot. Dan would soon be joining us to begin setting up his lighting gear. You don't just start taking photographs. A lot of preparation is required. It is not an immediate flash of a camera shutter.

When Sophia opened the front door, her sheer presence made everything around her pale by comparison. It didn't matter that Ted had done a fabulous job, that the interiors reflected her elegance and grace, and were filled with many pieces of furniture and favorite objets d'art from her residences in Geneva and Rome. All I could see at the moment was Sophia's breathtaking beauty. She didn't have a stitch of makeup on, and her hair wasn't yet brushed out. She was wearing a robe. It didn't matter at all, and I got the feeling that wherever she went in the world, people found her as captivating as I did.

After warmly welcoming me, Sophia took me to her closet where she pulled out several different changes of clothing for the day's photo shoot. She asked my opinion about each outfit. Her sense of style was remarkable, and I told her so. She certainly didn't need to hear it from *me*.

It was apparent to me that she considered it a joy to be around water and in the sun, especially with her husband and children. That's one of the reasons why they had chosen Williams Island as one of their vacation retreats. Another was that the new community offered privacy, allowing her to lead a near-normal family life when she wasn't working. Plus, numerous resort amenities made up the Williams Island lifestyle—swimming pools, marinas for boating, tennis courts, a world-class spa, and dining facilities were within its gates. All of these factors pleased Sophia. They also pleased other international residents as well as those from within the United States, eventually leading to the successful sell-out of the community from its first through final phases.

The Pontis' permanent residence at the time was in Geneva, where their sons were still attending school. Sophia had told Ted Fine that she wanted him to recreate the relaxing atmosphere from that grand apartment in her South Florida condominium. A place to curl up in a cozy chair and wind down. Although there were many European influences in the new condo, she especially liked that the design was comfortable and efficient—things that are important to Americans. And I would discover that evening how much she enjoyed being in her modern American-style kitchen.

In Sophia's master suite, there was a very beautiful bed, which she had shipped from one of her European residences. I was extremely touched when she told me that, after having had two miscarriages, she was confined to bed rest in *that* bed, before she eventually gave birth to each of her and Carlo's sons. That bed meant a lot to her. I could see she had an emotional attachment to it.

The master bedroom also had a hammock, where Carlo oftentimes cat-napped. In addition, Sophia had an exquisite dressing table with a glass top. When I was admiring it, I noticed that there were photographs of both of their boys, from birth to the present time, tucked beneath the glass. As she proudly pointed out each child to me, I could tell how much she loved the real-life role of motherhood.

After Dan arrived, he took some Polaroid shots to make sure the lighting was right and there weren't any shadows. There were other things that a skilled photographer looks for too. For this purpose, he asked me to be Sophia's stand-in. So I pretended that I was her (as best as I could!) and posed in various locations. I didn't mind doing this at all, because I knew this would be a great story to tell my family and friends.

Meanwhile, Sophia was getting dressed into one of her outfits. She did her own hair and makeup. She was not a prima donna at all.

After Dan had finished snapping the Polaroids, Sophia and I both sat crossed-legged on the floor in the living room and viewed them. We made some comments before the actual photo shoot started. My eye glasses were resting on the bridge of my nose as I spoke.

Sophia noticed them. In 1980 she had launched her own eyewear brand—a collection of prescription optical frames with the style and glamour of the movie star herself. This made sense since Sophia Loren was known the world over for her exquisite cat eyes, not just for her sensual, voluptuous body—*or* talent.

"I love your eyeglasses, Maxine."

"Sophia, these are just over-the-counter magnifiers," I said, laughing.

"They are so beautiful!" she told me.

"I usually buy these reading glasses at the Festival Flea Market in Pompano Beach. Three pairs for fifteen dollars."

"This cannot be!" she said.

"Honestly, Sophia. *These* particular glasses might have cost a little bit more. Maybe they were ten dollars rather than five dollars apiece. And I got them at JC*Pennaaaaaay*," I informed her, trying to replicate a French accent as best as I could. "Here. *You* keep them." I handed them to her.

"Oh no, Maxine! I couldn't possibly take them from you!" she responded. She apparently thought they were very stylish.

"Please, Sophia. Take them. Enjoy them." I was practically begging. "Believe me. I will be paid back every time I tell this story to other people. I'll probably tell it hundreds of times."

I finally convinced her to accept the glasses. She was so sincerely grateful that you would have thought I had given her the Hope Diamond.

And I *have* told that story hundreds of times. But this is the first time I have actually put it in writing. It truly is one of my all-time favorite stories.

After Dan finished shooting for the day, Sophia asked me to stay for dinner. She tossed some pasta into a pot of boiling water, whipped up some sauce, and voilà! Although it wasn't eggplant parmigiana, one of her specialties (and mine too), it might as well have been. There we were, sitting in her kitchen, chatting away like two old college chums. No pretense. Just being giddy and "girly." The entire experience was surreal and extraordinary to me.

Sophia Loren was born Sofia Villani Scicolone in Rome and had a war-torn childhood. As our conversation continued, we discovered that we had the same birth date—September 21, in the *same year*. We were exactly the same age! Believe me, if there were other similarities, they would have been a fluke.

At this time, Sophia was working less frequently because she wanted to be close to home while raising her sons, Carlo Jr. and Edoardo. In fact, in 1981 she reportedly turned down the role of the vengeful Alexis Carrington in the *Dynasty* television series. Instead, English actress Joan Collins got the part. I think only Sophia could have done that and remained unfazed.

She also turned down a marriage proposal from Cary Grant when they both starred in *The Pride and The Passion* in 1957. Instead, she chose Carlo Ponti, twenty two years her senior, who became her mentor, best friend, husband, career manager, and father figure. If she had any regrets, I certainly could not detect them.

On the following days, we carried out the same routine in Sophia's Williams Island condominium until Dan had completed the *Architectural Digest* photo shoot assignment. I only joined Sophia for dinner on that first night. I wanted to continue my ritual of having dinner with my husband every night of our married life, with very few exceptions.

Postscript: While doing some research about Sophia for this book, I found several websites that quote her as having said, "Spaghetti can be eaten most successfully if you inhale it like a vacuum cleaner." FYI: On that first evening, we both did.

CHAPTER 9

My-T-Fine

The Adler Network served Ted Fine of Fine Decorators for nearly two decades. We represented Ted longer than any other client. His design studio, which later was renamed Home of Fine Decorators, was located off I-95 and Hallandale Beach Boulevard in Broward County. During those years, my learning curve about the design industry skyrocketed. He taught me much more than I had ever known before.

Our meetings were weekly, held every Tuesday for a minimum of two hours. Ted, one of my writers, and I discussed new ideas and marketing strategies and read through what we had written. We shared the most recent publicity clips about Ted and his company. We also interviewed him for new press releases or feature stories. Ted never took a call during those meetings, because he wanted our focus to be entirely on him. It was.

Before Ted retained our agency, when he was just starting out in business, he had a partner. The partner's daughter had a husband who wanted to learn the design business. So they took the son-in-law in and taught him everything he needed to know. The son-in-law was Steven Gurowitz who, years later, went out on his own. He established Interiors by Steven G, an interior design company that subsequently became very successful, just as Fine Decorators had done.

I recall there being tremendous rivalry between Ted and Steven after that. It was like a law at Fine Decorators: Never mention Steven's name in front of Ted. So I was surprised when Mitchel Fine, Ted's son, recently told me that Steven attributes much of his own success to Ted Fine. Home furnishings representatives had mentioned this to Mitchel and he passed that information along to me. Yet, when I looked at Interiors by Steven G's website, there was no mention of a prior working relationship with Ted.

Ted's business relationship with the Soffer family from Turnberry Isles Yacht & Country Club as well as with the Trump family from Williams Island elevated Ted to the status of South Florida's premier designer. He had the lion's share of everything in those exclusive Aventura condominium communities and beyond.

At Turnberry, Ted was involved from the ground up with the layout of the apartments. He took the developer's drawings and floor plans and worked with architects to alter them in order to meet the needs and lifestyle requirements of Turnberry buyers. It was only as a favor that Ted would furnish the interiors of a buyer's residence there. He did, however, design many of Turnberry's models and the common areas of its buildings.

Ted hired our agency to represent and publicize him. For the most part, this was an "easy do" because he was doing furnished model residences at Williams Island, the common areas of the high-rise buildings, and a lot of residences owned by celebrity buyers. He was highly respected for his firm's design work, and there was great teamwork between him and the developers, Jules, Stephanie and Eddie Trump.

SHOWMANSHIP

When you walked into Fine Decorators, you passed by the receptionist and entered the design studio, where you were bowled over. There was a raised platform that held about half a dozen tables. Ted and one of his firm's interior designers sat with a prospective client or a client who was already on board, and conducted a very impressive project presentation. Ted had a fabulous gal working for him who did all of the renderings (drawings) back then. There were many pages of renderings, color boards, and fabric swatches to excite clients. Ted was masterful at these presentations. He also dropped the names of the celebrities who had hired his firm to design the interiors of their residences, which further enticed them. Not only had Ted worked for these stars, but he hobnobbed with them too. That was the truth.

At the same time that one presentation was taking place, others were taking place as well. Everything was perfectly timed so that Fine Decorators always looked busy. After all, who would want to work with a firm that had no other clients? This was great showmanship and a great marketing strategy.

Actors Sophia Loren, Lucille Ball, James Caan, and Burt Reynolds, along with singer Whitney Houston, tennis professionals Jimmy Connors and Vitas Gerulaitis, slugger Sammy Sosa, and other celebrities hired Ted's firm to design the interiors of their residences. So did high-profile clients such as Dr. Barth Green, president of the Miami Project to Cure Paralysis, and criminal defense attorney Roy Black following his marriage to Lisa Lea Haller. I visited those residences many times because the Adler Network was writing stories about them.

I'd be remiss if I didn't say a few words about Roy and Lea Black's historic, Mediterranean-style estate home in Coral Gables. It was originally built in 1924 by the founder of that city, George Merrick; the Blacks later renovated it. The result was spectacular. I was in that home about four or five times. I can still remember the first time I walked into the master bedroom and saw their wall sconces. I stopped short and took a double-take. Owen and I had the exact same sconces in our master bedroom. But, I assure you, the similarity stopped there! I can also still envision Lea's huge walk-in *lingerie* closet! I would have given anything to have had one a fraction of that size. And, because Roy was a prolific reader, there were built-in floor-to-ceiling bookshelves just about everywhere in that amazing home.

The Blacks were a great couple. Oftentimes called "The Professor" by his colleagues and students, Roy met Lea when she was a juror during the William Kennedy Smith rape trial in 1991. Roy was responsible for Smith's acquittal, and it catapulted him into the national spotlight. He and Lea were married in 1995. Roy went on to represent other well-known personalities, including radio talk show host Rush Limbaugh, artist Peter Max, actor Kelsey Grammer, NFL player Dennis Rodman, sportscaster Marv Albert, singer Justin Bieber, and others. Because Roy was highly respected in his profession, he also became a sought-after television legal analyst during criminal trial proceedings of high visibility, such as the O. J. Simpson trial. As for Lea, she could hold her own. She was an entrepreneur in the beauty business and went on to become one of the female stars in the reality TV series *Real Housewives of Miami*.

In the eighties, Ted, his design studio, along with his house and yacht (named *My-T-Fine* after the pudding brand that he loved but couldn't find in South Florida) were featured on Robin Leach's *Lifestyles of the Rich and Famous*. In 2004, Ted, his residence, and the Home of Fine Decorators appeared on VH1's *World's Most Expensive Homes*. The coverage included a tour of Ted's company headquarters. At that time, he probably had about eighty people working for him.

NOT SO FINE

In my opinion Ted had a complex personality. I never knew what mood he might be in, and sometimes I walked on eggshells not to wake up a sleeping giant. But he was a gifted businessman whom I admired.

Ted could be very charismatic when he was out in public at an event. Behind closed doors, I often thought he was self-absorbed, manipulative, and a bully. But I stuck with him because it was good for the Adler Network to say that we represented South Florida's top interior design firm. When he was at the pinnacle of his career, his name was like a magnet that attracted other designers to our agency as clients. They too wanted the recognition that Ted was getting. I will always be grateful for that.

What I'm really saying is that the back of the house was sometimes very different from the front of the house, particularly when it came to Ted's treatment of the interior designers who worked for him. While Ted's clients loved him, I think his designers felt differently about him. Robert Perlberg, Richard Nemec, and Arnold Schulman were among them, and my heart oftentimes went out to them. I was present on several occasions when Ted called them in, took out their design boards for a project, and harshly criticized them. It wasn't because their design wasn't good. It *was* good. But it was my impression that Ted might have been a little paranoid, thinking they were selling *their own* designs rather than the designs of Fine Decorators. (Ted had, after all, been smart enough to hire them, so shouldn't *he* get the credit?) Those talented designers appeared to be intimated by their boss, but they didn't speak up for fear of losing the jobs they needed. I think they also felt that Ted might compromise their reputations in the industry.

Likewise, Ted was frequently critical of and rude to the Adler Network's male writer who was assigned to his account. I believe there are nice ways to dole out criticism. You don't have to demean a person the way Ted frequently did.

He could also be temperamental with me. One particular incident stands out in my mind.

Ted dressed to the nines, as if he had just stepped out of a page from *Gentlemen's Quarterly*. He was fastidious, always striving to look impeccable, polished and well coifed. And he succeeded. He made an impressive appearance.

Ted's hair, in particular, was something he was very finicky about. One day, after I had arranged for a meeting with us at the Boca Raton Resort and Club, we drove together and valet parked at the Pink Tower. As we started to walk toward the building, Ted's hair began blowing every which way in the wind. He wasn't a happy camper. He became very angry and reprimanded me, saying that I knew there was a wind tunnel in that location, and I had purposely brought him there. Well, I certainly did *not* know we'd be walking through a wind tunnel. And *if* I had known, how could I have avoided it so Ted wouldn't have become upset? It was just *hair,* for Pete's sake. But hair was apparently a big issue for Ted.

So was getting his hands dirty. Dirt was incompatible with the perfect physical appearance he always maintained. Ted could be a little Howard Hughes–ish because he avoided germs at all costs. (Actually, I shouldn't throw stones. As I grew older, I began taking precautions to avoid germs too.)

Another flashback takes me inside of Ted and his wife Jeannette's fabulous Keystone Point home overlooking Biscayne Bay in North Miami. It was very modern and had a large dramatic winding staircase. I was talking with their son, Mitchel, when their daughter, Rhonda, walked in with a new puppy. The dog went to the bathroom on the carpeting on the stairs, and both siblings hurried to clean it up. I think they were concerned about what their father would say if he saw it. They apparently did not want to find out. It was hilarious to watch them perform the fastest poop-scoop job I had ever seen!

I don't think this would have bothered Jeannette as much. The Fines had an Airedale terrier and a poodle. Jeannette also was tremendously committed to the work being done by the Humane Society. And when the *Sun-Sentinel* once interviewed her about sharing a home with one or more dogs, she explained that the black, brown, and tan color scheme in their residence matched the colors of their dogs. Apparently, she and Ted had purposely selected those colors. She said she didn't care if the dogs scratched their leather sofas. So my gut tells me that it was Ted who had a lot less tolerance.

I *did*, however, hear from Mitchel that his dad lightened up about the dogs as the years passed.

Still, Ted always liked to keep his house in order. When he came home from work, he went outside on the back terrace and realigned any pieces of patio furniture that had been blown out of place from the wind. A small confession: *I* do the same thing!

Working with Ted was never boring. If I ever were to need an Ativan or Xanax, it would have been during the years I represented him. As an example, one day I received a call from Joan Fleischman, the gossip columnist from the *Miami Herald*. She called to give me a heads up about an item she would be running in her "Talk of Our Town" column the next day. Ted's daughter, Rhonda, was going through a very nasty divorce. Her husband was cleaning out their home and taking more than his own belongings, including diaper bags. Joan said that Ted had chased his son-and-law down and confronted him.

I was glad to have had that information in advance from a media colleague. Joan obviously respected me and wanted me to prepare for any backlash that might follow. But I already was aware of what had occurred. I had been like an aunt to the Fine kids over the years and was privy to much of went on in both of their lives.

When I told Ted about the article that Joan planned to publish, he insisted that I stop the presses and kill it.

I was good at many things. But in reality, it's only in the movies that you can stop the presses. It was beyond my capabilities.

That hadn't been the first or the last time that Ted would be the subject of Joan's column. So, like I said, this particular client account was always a fascinating one, with many challenges to overcome.

VERY FINE

Ted had married his high school sweetheart. Jeannette was a beautiful red-head, but Ted frequently seemed to be concerned about her physical appearance. He never wanted her to gain weight. I thought that was a lot of pressure to put on one's spouse, but he did it anyway. I do remember that, years later, Jeannette underwent cosmetic surgery. Ted and I were meeting her at the Island Club at Williams Island for an event. Her face was still a little puffy, and she had hidden most of her hair beneath a white turban. But she looked absolutely stunning. I gave her a lot of credit for being brave enough to go out in public just a few days following the surgical procedure.

Ted and Jeannette were very philanthropic. Mitchel reminded me that Ted had been among the founders of Mt. Sinai Hospital in Miami Beach. The Fines also supported the Miami Jewish Home and Hospital for the Aged at Douglas Gardens in Miami, as well as Temple Beth Moshe Hebrew Day School in North Miami. They were generous donors to the Humane Society of Greater Miami, JAFCO (Jewish Adoption & Foster Care Options), the Sylvester Comprehensive Cancer Center in Miami, and other charitable organizations too.

Ted also financially backed Mitchel in business when Mitchel decided to leave medical school.

"I had lied to myself that I always wanted to be a doctor. I woke up one day in med school and realized I hated it. So my dad presented me with an alternative," Mitchel told me.

"My dad had great foresight. He knew that Aventura was densely populated and that people no longer were going to the Miami Design District or up to West Palm Beach to shop for home furnishings. He put up the money, enabling me to open the first showroom at DCOTA (the Design Center of the Americas) in Dania."

That showroom was (and still is) Judith Norman. I discuss it in greater detail in chapter 15.

For reasons I prefer not to share, after approximately nineteen years of being a loyal spokesperson for Ted Fine, I resigned his account. My letter of resignation to him was the second of three letters of resignation I wrote to clients during my career.

I've heard that Ted currently spends half the year in a double unit at the Fontainebleau on Miami Beach and the other half of the year in an apartment in La Costa, near San Diego, California. I'm certain the interiors are beautiful. I am truly glad for him and harbor no ill feelings. When we worked together, we had a great ride!

CHAPTER 10

The Great Gatsby

WHAT DID *THE GREAT GATSBY*, the 1925 novel by F. Scott Fitzgerald, have to do with one of Boca Raton's most prestigious country club communities? It became the theme for its advertising and marketing campaigns.

The community I'm referring to is St. Andrews County Club.

But unlike that book, which didn't become successful until decades after its publication, St. Andrews was an immediate triumph for its developer, Jerry Ansel. At one point, St. Andrews boasted nearly $16 million in sales in just one month. This was truly remarkable because home prices at that time hadn't yet appreciated to today's prices. Back in the eighties and early nineties, the least expensive new homes offered there were in the $350,000 to $450,000 range.

When Jerry brought our public relations agency on board at St. Andrews, we worked with him and John Csapo, the executive vice president. Others whom I remember were Ronald Reitsma, the broker of record for the community; John Thomson, vice president of sales and marketing; and John's wife, sales associate Connie Thomson. There was a terrific group to market this exciting project.

John Thomson knew a lot about marketing and was a genius at it. (He had worked at J. Walter Thompson Advertising in New York.) So "The Great Gatsby" advertising theme he implemented was very innovative. Even the grand opening event at St. Andrews was orchestrated on a grand scale, including fireworks. I'm sure that Jay Gatsby would have been proud.

The campaign wasn't about excess or decadence. Instead, it focused on the pursuit of happiness through a seductive and enviable lifestyle. Even though

St. Andrews wasn't built during the era of the Roaring Twenties with its flap-
per culture, jazz music, and bootlegging, this new community emerged when
real estate development was thriving in South Florida, during the eighties. It
was an exciting time, and the homes at St. Andrews became a reward for a life
well lived.

As the creative mastermind behind this new community, and as president
of the St. Andrews Development Corp. of Boca, Jerry Ansel laid a foundation
for the ultimate in fine living from the onset. He imagined single-family estate
homes, with a minimum of thirty-five hundred square feet each, on one-acre
lots set against a picturesque landscape. The low-density, 657-acre community
would be limited to no more than 657 residences. As it turned out, there were
fewer homes than that because some buyers built on more than one lot.

There would also be an array of world-class recreational and cultural
amenities coupled with flawless service. Two-thirds of the community was
reserved for outdoor recreational use. Plans included two championship golf
courses, sixteen tennis courts, a croquet greensward, swimming pool, and a
luxurious full-service clubhouse.

The St. Andrews style was designed to reflect the shared tastes and in-
terests of its refined members. After sales began, and to demonstrate the sophistication of St. Andrews' club life, recognizable talent could sometimes
be found entertaining buyers at the community. Italian-born composer Gian
Carlo Menotti directed a symphony on the golf course, and journalist and
actor George Plimpton told some of his favorite stories at St. Andrews. The
community hosted the 1983 Designer Showcase Home of the North Broward
Society of the Symphony at a $1.4 million estate. Charities frequently raise
funds in this way. Their patrons and other supporters pay admission to visit
these beautifully furnished "showcase" homes. Simultaneously, this benefits
the host community that is selling new homes by bringing in prospective
buyers.

Jerry brought in many of South Florida's premier home builders to construct residences of distinctive character and enduring quality at St. Andrews.
Curtis House, who owned Direct Interiors and was an Adler Network client, created the interiors of many of those builders' palatial model homes.

That relationship worked out well. When we publicized St. Andrews Country Club, we oftentimes wrote about Direct Interiors. When we publicized Direct Interiors, we oftentimes mentioned St. Andrews. *It was a win for both of those clients.*

Instead of paying governmental impact fees, Jerry opted to extend Jog Road (known as Powerline Road to the south) from Yamato north to Clint Moore. This stretch of roadway alleviated traffic problems and also contributed to the further development of western Boca Raton.

While developing his community, Jerry sold his company to Broadview Savings and Loan Association and Cuyahoga Savings and Loan Company of Cleveland. They acquired sixty acres next to the St. Andrews site to extend St. Andrews. None of these changes impinged on St. Andrews' luxury orientation or its growth. And Jerry stayed very involved. In fact, he was like the mayor of St. Andrews. If this was a movie, he'd be right on script.

To me, what spoke volumes about the quality of St. Andrews was that Jerry and his wife Ester lived there. As you know, you can't escape your neighbors. So Jerry was very confident in the product and lifestyle he was creating. He was always present as the community progressed according to his master plan. He inspired and influenced every developmental phase to ensure that St. Andrews would provide continuity from the time the first shovel of dirt came out of the ground, through its completion and sellout in the early nineties. It became a vibrantly active and social private membership community, not to mention a community of extremely high social prominence.

Jerry was a fascinating man, with a bundle of "way, way out" ideas. When he came up with one of those far-fetched concepts, even if it had nothing to do with St. Andrews, he didn't think twice about calling me at 3:00 a.m. He'd run his idea by me and ask what I thought about it. For the most part, those ideas were beyond grandiose! They were so far off the charts that on the one hand I became excited thinking "We can do this." His obsession became my obsession. On the other hand, I questioned, "How could anyone even be *thinking* of doing this?" Furthermore, he expected me or someone else to make it happen! His ideas were so dauntingly challenging that they were impossible to carry out. And I am not one to believe in *impossible.* But they truly were either unattainable or unachievable. One idea had to do with a huge event Jerry wanted to hold in the Northeast United States. But the logistics, along with all of the other factors, made it truly out of the question to bring to fruition. Nevertheless, you had to admire the guy for his out-of-the-box thinking. And this was before "out of the box" became a popular phrase.

Jerry told me that President George H. W. Bush was his good buddy. He had stories to tell after he had been invited to the senior Bush's home in Kennebunkport, Maine, to stay with him and First Lady Barbara Bush. Jerry also made it sound as if the President wouldn't do anything without *his* approval first. He was a financial supporter of the senior Bush too. I never asked my client if he wanted, or hoped for, an ambassadorship! I doubt it because he was very good, and successful, being a real estate developer.

As St. Andrews grew, Jerry formed St. Andrews Country Club Realty, which became the brokerage of choice for original residents at St. Andrews who were putting their homes on the market. He presided over the company, playing a dominant role in the marketing of those resales. Ronald Reitsma headed up the sales associates team, which included some of the residents of the community.

Jerry also had the ability to help homeowners who later wanted to renovate rather than relocate. With his in-depth knowledge of the St. Andrews lifestyle, he was ideally poised to handle design and construction through his separate general contracting firm. That was a great option for those homeowners.

Jerry had a golden touch, and the creation of his vision was commendable. Through the years, St. Andrews Country Club has been credited with having put the northwest quadrant of Boca Raton on the map as the nucleus of coveted real estate. It has matured into a lively year-round community. Moreover, St. Andrews has been recognized as a Distinguished Emerald Club of the World and a Platinum Club of America Five-Star Private Club. It also is also among Top Ten Healthiest Clubs in America.

While writing this book, we looked online and discovered that the *Great Gatsby* theme hadn't been forgotten. The exclusive private club community held a *Great Gatsby* event just a few years ago. It was gratifying for me to know that St. Andrews' advertising and marketing campaign has lived on for three decades.

Several years ago, my associate Judy Goldstein and I had the privilege of touring the St. Andrews home of Billi and Bernie Marcus, benefactors of the Marcus Neuroscience Institute at Boca Raton Regional Hospital. Bernie had been the cofounder of the Home Depot. We were representing designer Louis Shuster at the time, and Louis had created their residential interiors. I still can remember the *two* tables in the dining room and the pneumatic vacuum elevator in Bernie's study. Instead of cables or pulleys, a vacuum is used to lift the cab. It was pretty amazing…and don't get me started on the size of the Marcuses' expansive wardrobe closets! They were the size of bedrooms. Upstairs, there was an entire wing designed for their visiting children and grandchildren.

St. Andrews wasn't Jerry Ansel's first development or his last. Another of his notable properties was a beachfront condominium, the St. James, on Longboat Key on the west coast of Florida. And when he later offered the upscale single-family home community of Stonebrook Estates in Davie (in western Broward County), I'm happy to say that the Adler Network was right by his side.

Postscript: Following the sellout of St. Andrews, John and Connie Thomson went to work for Canada Square, the Toronto-based company that had acquired control of the remaining undeveloped land at Woodfield Country Club in Boca Raton from Resolution Trust Corp. (George Barbar had been the original developer, but he went belly up in 1992.) Canada Square appointed John as the head of sales and marketing at Woodfield, and Connie became a valued sales associate. So, years later, when the Adler Network became Woodfield's PR agency of record, I again worked with them. This represented a new chapter in the evolution of Woodfield. At that time, developer Bobby Julien was only in his twenties and stood at the helm of Canada Square, which later became Kolter.

Likewise, we represented Kolter and worked with the Thomsons a third time when the development of PGA Village in Port St. Lucie was under way. (The Thomsons, however, were not involved much later, at the time we worked with Kolter to help market Verano in Port St. Lucie.)

Relationships can *be long lasting, as ours were.*

CHAPTER 11

To the White House

Macramé is a form of art, and we learned a lot about it when we were hired in the late eighties to promote and publicize Macramates, a business owned by Steve and Joan Weinberg in Fort Lauderdale.

Thought to have originated with thirteenth-century Arabian weavers, the art of decorating with knots was a wildly popular item in home furnishings in the modern world during the late seventies and a portion of the eighties. Macramé, in the form of wall hangings, plant hangers, towels, tablecloths, window treatments, and other items have evolved and continue to be sold today. Nowadays these items are more sophisticated and use many more types of fibers.

The Weinbergs developed a thriving business serving the interior design trade. Applying their innovative concepts in fiber art for the home, they could custom design almost anything if you brought them an idea. Otherwise, you could make selections from their own creations, which were vibrantly colored fiber showpieces.

So what does macramé have to do with the White House?

Very Special Arts

The couple had created a fiber logo for the Kennedy Center's Very Special Arts. This came about because Joan's brother Herb worked with Iowa-based Newton Manufacturing, the maker of specialty advertising and promotional items. Newton was producing items with the Very Special Arts (VSA) logo.

That was what led Owen and me to 1600 Pennsylvania Avenue NW in Washington, DC, during the George H. W. Bush Administration. An invitation arrived at our home from the forty-first President of the United States and First Lady Barbara Bush, requesting our presence at a VSA day-time event in the Rose Garden at the White House in June 1989, followed by an evening at the Kennedy Center. We were thrilled and grateful that Macramates had submitted our name to the White House to be included on the guest list.

VSA was a global organization involved with the arts, education and the disabled. Founded in 1974 by Jean Kennedy Smith as the National Committee–Arts for the Handicapped and headquartered in the nation's capital, the organization was renamed Very Special Arts in 1985. My guess is that Jean Kennedy Smith (a daughter of Joseph and Rose Kennedy) was motivated to help people with disabilities because her sister, Rosemary Kennedy, had been born with a disability that worsened over the years.

The organization's mission was to provide persons with disabilities with the opportunity to learn, participate in, and enjoy the arts. Each year, millions of disabled persons of all ages and from all walks of life were able to benefit from VSA's education programs, including those for the visual and literary arts, as well as for dance, music, and theater. (In 2011, VSA merged with the Kennedy Center's Office on Accessibility. This led to another name change, from VSA to the Department of VSA and Accessibility at the John F. Kennedy Center for the Performing Arts.)

Arriving in the Rose Garden in 1989, Owen and I were greeted by marines in white uniforms standing at attention, as well as jets flying in unison overhead. I got goose bumps and never felt prouder to be an American. Every time I recall this occasion, my eyes well up with tears. I'm a copious crier when it comes to all things patriotic.

The first row of seating had been reserved for the Kennedy family and other dignitaries, and we were overjoyed to be sitting directly behind them in a continuation of the VIP area. I will never understand why *we* too had ringside seats at that VSA presentation at the White House. Rest assured, we did not complain.

Among recognizable Kennedy family members present that day were Ethel Kennedy and Eunice Kennedy Shriver and her husband Sargent Shriver. He had been the driving force behind the Peace Corps. We also were in the company of celebrities, such as singer Kenny Rogers.

That evening we were entertained with performances by disabled children and adults at the Kennedy Center. How they had overcome their handicaps in order to master a form of the performing arts was truly astounding. We wouldn't have enjoyed this more had an A-list of celebrities been on stage instead.

A TRIBUTE TO THE WORLD'S CHILDREN

In 1992, the graceful and elegant actress Audrey Hepburn came to Fort Lauderdale to participate in "A Tribute to the World's Children" fundraiser. It was a UNICEF production held at the Broward Center for the Performing Arts. Hepburn, UNICEF's Goodwill Ambassador, was joined by the energetic Lisa Minelli and hundreds of child dancers. Veteran choreographer June Taylor had coached a cast of four hundred fifty kids from the tricounty area who performed that evening to rave reviews. (Her *adult* June Taylor Dancers had performed regularly during the sixties on the *Jackie Gleason Show*. That popular CBS television program had been videotaped at the Miami Beach Auditorium. Today that venue is called the Jackie Gleason Theater.)

On that special evening at the Broward Center, Hepburn dispelled the myth that everyone loves children. She pointed out that forty thousand children die each day. Along with receiving no love, they have no rights and no care. She urged people in the audience to make donations to UNICEF to help those forgotten youth.

The Brussels-born Hepburn, who had grown up in Holland during the Nazi occupation, revealed that she herself had been undernourished, asthmatic, and anemic during her own childhood. But her home had been filled with love and life. That made a world of difference. As you can imagine, her speech was a tear jerker. She was truly a humanitarian, earning just one dollar a year from the worldwide organization to serve as its Goodwill Ambassador.

Another poignant moment came when Steve and Joan Weinberg ascended the stage to present Hepburn with a large fiber mural they had created especially for the occasion. It depicted children of all races and ethnicities.

Owen and I were proud to be seated in the audience on that evening.

WHITE HOUSE'S TWO HUNDREDTH ANNIVERSARY

Once again, the Adler Network enjoyed a connection to the White House when we were hired by Newton Manufacturing to announce that they would be the exclusive supplier of merchandise to commemorate the two hundredth anniversary of the White House in 2000. The sale of wearables, pens, computer mouse pads, mugs, and more than two hundred thousand other items would benefit millions of American students. In addition to disseminating a press release about this, we produced the brochure for this special merchandising program. It was targeted at American corporations and organizations. By purchasing promotional items with the "White House 200th Anniversary" logo, a portion from the sale of every item was earmarked directly for educational programs in schools in all fifty states, the District of Columbia, our US territories, and the Department of Defense schools overseas.

The programs for our nation's youth would include the study of the White House and its role in the culture of freedom and democracy that is uniquely American. Students would be encouraged to compose and perform music in their schools and communities, as well as create works of visual art. Following state and regional competition, selected winners would be recognized by demonstrating their musical or artistic talents during a concert and exhibition at the White House celebration, starting in November 2000.

Newton Manufacturing's "pitch" was also that companies and organizations could have their logo alongside the "White House 200th Anniversary" logo, and give the promotional items away to their customers, clients, suppliers, associates, or employees. As a marketing tool for themselves, these items would strengthen their credibility and image.

The two hundredth anniversary hoopla took place over a two-year period, during the Bill Clinton administration.

No. Owen and I weren't invited back to the White House. But I was okay with that. My patriotic spirit continued—and still does—no matter what.

CHAPTER 12

East Meets West

SEVERAL REAL ESTATE DEVELOPERS WITH whom we worked were planning luxury condominium projects that never got off the ground. The timing might have been wrong. There could have been an unexpected downturn in the market. They may not have been able to secure financing. Or other reasons. Azure in Highland Beach, CityClub Residences in Boca Raton, The Waves Las Olas in Fort Lauderdale, and Domani in North Palm Beach were among them.

PRESIDENTIAL PLACE

We did, however, represent one project where construction had begun, stopped, then started up again and became a sell-out success several years later. This was only possible, I believe, because of the man who created and presided over that project. His name—John Temple.

John, a past president of the Arvida Corporation, had admired a particular parcel of land since the time Arvida owned the Boca Raton Resort and Club. Overlooking the ocean to the east and Lake Boca Raton to the west and situated on resort grounds just north of the Boca Beach Club, the land was a prime piece of real estate.

John expected the resort to expand and build additional hotel rooms on the site, but this never happened. Meanwhile, VMS Realty had purchased the resort from Arvida in 1983.

After John left Arvida, he formed a partnership with VMS Realty of Chicago and became president and managing partner of VMS/Temple

Development. The project they jointly planned to develop was on that choice parcel, which they had acquired. Presidential Place would be a forty-two-unit, seven-story building with condominiums ranging in size from four thousand seven hundred to ten thousand square feet. The smallest unit would be larger than most single-family homes! Four- and five-bedroom floor plans would be offered at prices starting from $1.45 million, or close to $300 per square foot. That was indeed a bargain for new *oceanfront* property back in the springtime of 1989, when sales at Presidential Place began.

While John had been with Arvida, he developed the Addison ocean-front condominium in Boca Raton during the mid eighties. Condos went for $150 to $160 per square foot. At the time that Presidential Place began selling, resales in the Addison were fetching between $350 and $400 per square foot.

Presidential Place promised to be the new pinnacle of excellence in care-free luxury living in Boca Raton. Each residence would provide private, keyed elevator access, spectacular water views, and a private beach cabana, to name a few of the selling features. The on-site beach cabana in itself was highly at-tractive; it would have a wet bar, refrigerator and ice machine, shower, water closet, and wiring for telephone and cable television services. This was before people had cellular phones, which meant that buyers at Presidential Place could stay connected while being just steps from a pool or seven hundred feet of Atlantic shoreline.

Another benefit of living there would be that vendors, such as dry clean-ers, grocers, and caterers, could enter an owner's residence into the laundry room via the private elevator. (Doors to the elevator opened both ways.) They wouldn't have to arrive at the front door and walk through the condo to reach the kitchen or laundry room. This concept was something relatively new to the real estate industry, much like a private beach cabana was. Furthermore, residents could take their elevator directly down to the ocean level to their cabanas. This was convenience with a capital *C*.

John also offered prospective buyers the ability to customize their interi-ors to meet their individual needs and tastes and had the professionals ready to do it. These units wouldn't be *same old, same old* by any means.

Although the project would set a new standard for oceanfront luxury, there was one fly in the ointment. The drawback was the entrance. When you came off A1A (South Ocean Boulevard) and drove toward Presidential Place, you were on the same path as you would take to reach the Boca Raton Resort and Club's Boca Beach Club. So there would be a lot of traffic to contend with. To counteract this, and to turn a negative into a positive, we touted the benefits of a private Premier Club resort membership and *included* that membership and first-year dues with each condominium purchase. (That's when a membership was valued at $18,000.) As a result, Presidential Place residents could enjoy the many amenities and services offered at the main resort and its beach club, such as housekeeping and hotel room service in their own residence. Imagine being able to pick up a phone and soon be enjoying bagels or croissants on your private terrace or by your own poolside cabana! If desired, a resort shuttle bus would take residents to and from Presidential Place and the Boca Beach Club or the main resort and even to Mizner Park in the downtown area. Plus, Mizner's Dream (the resort's water taxi) was available to shuttle them back and forth across Lake Boca Raton. A cushy lifestyle was there for the taking, if you could afford it.

Within six weeks of putting the Presidential Place condos on the market, there were eighteen purchase offers, after each buyer had plopped down a reservation payment of $100,000 to prove he or she was serious. John Temple had spent very little money on advertising. A shovel hadn't yet gone into the ground. There was, quite simply, a demand. And that summer, I recall John telling a *Sun-Sentinel* reporter that it is never "off season" when selling million-dollar oceanfront condominiums. I couldn't have agreed more. It always drove me nuts when other developers only wanted to market their projects during the South Florida "season" because northern snowbirds were in town. In reality, purchasers of high-end residences have the means to buy at *any* time. They can hop on an airplane for a day or two, if needed. Quite often, it is not between November and April. Many sales are made over the summer months.

I found it truly fascinating to work with John, one of the brightest men I had ever known. If my recollection is right, he had been a submarine captain during World War II. He was a consummate professional, and it was always a privilege and a joy to be in his company. During meetings, he demonstrated his savvy and understood the value of marketing and public relations. He recognized the power of the written word like I did.

Things were going along great until the early nineties when VMS experienced dire cash flow problems. Consequently, construction on Presidential Place was halted in its early stages. VMS also put the Boca Raton Resort and Club up for sale.

Construction on the new condominium building remained dormant for several years.

A decline in the real estate market from 1989 into the early nineties didn't help matters. This left John Temple in a bind. But he wasn't one to just sit around. He was a doer.

John was looking for a new partner to replace VMS. Don't ask me why, but one day I just happened to mention Naples, Florida-based Collier Enterprises. All I knew about the company was that real estate was its main source of wealth. Founded in 1911, it had been largely responsible for the creation of Collier County during the twenties. It was a large land owner and developer in western Florida. I also was aware that the Collier family was on the 1991 *Forbes* list of wealthiest US families, with a $1 billion net worth. Perhaps they would invest some of that wealth in Presidential Place. It wouldn't hurt to wish or to *ask*.

I'll spare you all of the details and give you the Cliff Notes version. After John contacted that company, a deal was struck. Temple Development, with Collier Enterprises as its new partner, was able to acquire the delayed Presidential Place project for $10 million. Believe me, that was a steal. I think John had valued the project at between $50 million and $75 million when he first introduced it in 1989.

Why did a company on the west coast of Florida come to the rescue of one on Florida's east coast? It was an opportunity for Collier Enterprises to become established on the east coast with a showcase property. In fact, we wrote a multipage article with the headline "East Meets West," which appeared in a Palm Beach area glossy publication.

With VMS now out of the picture, John Temple and Collier Enterprises had to attract lenders back to Presidential Place. They needed construction financing and obtained it from ITT Real Estate Services of suburban Chicago. Consequently, in 1993, construction of the building started up again and the condos were put back on the market, starting *this* time from $1.6 million.

John, as CEO of Temple Development, had assembled a great group of professionals with a proven track record, including some from Arvida who had helped turn that company into one of Florida's leading real estate giants during the late seventies and eighties. Michael Post, a former Arvida vice president of construction, was named the chief operating officer at Presidential Place. He and John hired a first-rate construction team. O. W. "Woody" Woodard, who had been an associate of Arvida Realty Sales, became Presidential Place's sales manager.

Michael Post's strong suit was keeping all of the subcontractors in line. He was a stickler for getting things done right and getting them done on time and on budget. Because of his knowledge of construction, he often became involved in sales by showing prospective buyers around the building. He told them about everything they could and *couldn't* see—every last screw and nail and every nuance. Michael was a nuts-and-bolts kind of guy with a lot of passion for the project. People liked him and were confident that the building would be structurally sound.

The interior designers involved with Presidential Place had diverse talents and terrific credentials. They included Alfred Karram Jr., Judy Howard, and Terri Kennedy. Each designer furnished a model residence to demonstrate to prospective buyers how these condos could "live." Karram also was responsible for designing the common areas within the building. They were stunning, incorporating a lot of marble flooring, rich Italian-imported wood paneling, custom-colored carpeting, and an abundance of fine art. In addition, Karram purchased two residences in the building, and his firm created "turnkey" interiors that were ready for immediate occupancy. All a new resident had to do was bring clothes and a toothbrush.

Judy Howard of J/Howard Design also created the interiors of a beach cabana. The colorful, fun design was very avant-garde. We had a vertical photograph taken of it and were able to get it published, first on the cover of a national design magazine and then elsewhere. Again, a private beach cabana at a condominium was a new concept, so it attracted media interest.

And here's something that I think was a stroke of true generosity on John Temple's part. In December 1993, before the building was finished and occupied, he hired special effects artist Donald Moore. Working with Marco Rose of Miami Stage Lighting, they created a sophisticated and elegant holiday lighting scene. John wanted to share the holiday spirit and the building's festive façade with the local community. It was all aglow and very beautiful.

Since this was before I met Maxine, she did not know that I had been friends with Donald Moore in the late eighties. We were introduced by my cousin Barbara Brietstein, owner of the Social Register in Plantation. She called on Donald to create visuals for the parties she planned for her customers. Donald and I frequently played racquetball together in Plantation at the Sportroom Racquetball Health and Fitness Club. He was a great guy and a great talent.

By the time Presidential Place received its Certificate of Occupancy in 1994, nearly all of the forty-two condos had been sold. Soon after, there was a complete sellout. I believe the project, in spite of its problems, became a success because of the unified efforts on the part of the development, sales, and design teams. They did a stellar job.

A GOLDEN GIRL

In January 1994, after Presidential Place was completed, we decided to reach out to a charity, namely the Papanicolaou Women's Corps for Cancer Research. We offered the new building as the venue for their appreciation cocktail reception to thank designers and sponsors of a "Women of Design" art show scheduled the following month at DCOTA. The exhibit, which previously had appeared at the National Gallery in Washington, DC, would feature the works of thirty-two nationally recognized female architects and designers. The Women's Corps was going to help sponsor the DCOTA show in order to raise funds for the Sylvester Comprehensive Cancer Center at the University of Miami. The charitable organization also had plans for a fundraising gala.

American TV, film, and theater actress Estelle Getty was flying in from California to help the charity fight cancer. So we piggybacked off that opportunity to celebrate the grand opening of Presidential Place as well.

I picked up the tiny actress at the airport, only to see her shaking like a leaf. There had just been an earthquake in California, and it was very high on the Richter scale. That earthquake—the Northridge quake—rocked Los Angeles' San Fernando Valley, killing fifty-four people and causing billions of dollars in damages.

Rightly so, Getty was still a bundle of nerves from the natural disaster, until that evening when she appeared at Presidential Place. She was composed, calm, warm, and soft spoken. Or, *if* she was still flustered, she certainly didn't show it. Perhaps that was a reflection of her competent acting ability.

The Golden Globe– and Emmy Award–winner was nothing at all like Sicilian-born octogenarian Sophia Petrillo, the role she portrayed in the hit NBC television series *The Golden Girls*, which debuted in 1985. On that popular show, this delightful little woman was the sassy mother of Dorothy Zbornak, played by actress Bea Arthur. Getty's fictional character was much older than she actually was in real life. Betty White as Rose and Rue McClanahan as Blanche made up the remainder of the series' four main characters.

When Getty came to Presidential Place for the Papanicolaou Women's Corps event, she graciously posed for photographs and interacted with guests. Less than five feet tall, Getty was a giant when it came to being involved in worthy causes, among them cancer research and AIDs. It was a privilege to have met her.

The catering that evening was provided pro bono, if my memory serves me correctly, by Pete Boinis, owner of the popular Pete's Restaurant and Bar in Boca Raton. John Temple and Pete were close friends, and it had been John who encouraged Pete to open his restaurant at the Arvida Parkway Center off Glades Road years earlier when John was president of Arvida. So Pete agreed to help out at Presidential Place, and the food contributed to the lovely evening.

Limoncello

Aside from working professionally with the Presidential Place team, Owen and I got to know Michael Post and Judy Howard socially. They were dating each other at the time. They both encouraged us to go to Italy on vacation. We had never been to Europe, so we enthusiastically considered the idea. Also, now that Judy Goldstein was working with us, we felt confident that we could go away for more than just a long weekend (as we had done in the past), leave her in charge of the agency, and it would still be in good working order when we got back!

Michael laid out the terms of our trip in no uncertain terms. He insisted we only take a Tauck Tour and only purchase Tumi luggage. His third directive was that we must bring him back a bottle of limoncello from Sorrento. That was an Italian lemon liqueur.

We listened to everything Michael had told us. After we had booked our travel plans, he and Judy (Howard) then told us every place we should go, right down to the last detail about what we should eat in Italy. It was a real hoot.

Upon our arrival in Sorrento, the first thing we did was buy limoncello for Michael, and I schlepped it from hotel to hotel and from bus ride to bus ride. I didn't pack it in my bag or send it home. I carried that bottle around wherever we went throughout Italy. Owen would have killed me if he had not liked Michael as much as he did.

The best part of that trip was meeting a couple whose company we really enjoyed. The feeling was mutual, so the four of us went everywhere together. My recollection is that the husband was the editor of an International Monetary Fund publication, and his wife was in charge of DNA blood testing in Washington, DC. They lived in Chevy Chase, Maryland. They were knowledgeable, worldly, and interesting to be around. It was a real treat for us.

When we were with them in Venice, the wife recognized a beautiful Middle Eastern woman seated at a table next to us. They approached each other and kissed in the way Europeans do, on both cheeks. A moment later, Owen and I were introduced and discovered that she was royalty! We kissed one another in the same manner, and Owen even told her a joke.

The entire Italian experience was extraordinary. Of course, when we returned home to South Florida, I immediately delivered the bottle of limoncello, which was still fully intact, to Michael. Without knowing him, we never would have taken that memorable trip.

The following year, we took another Tauck tour. Along with the same couple we had met on the Italian tour, we traveled together throughout France.

CHAPTER 13

The Donald

IF YOU'VE EVER BEEN TO Palm Beach and had the opportunity to pass by or, better yet, visit Mar-a-Lago, it's likely to have left quite an impression. Built in the twenties by Marjorie Merriweather Post (then the wife of E. F. Hutton), the historic estate is situated between the Atlantic Ocean and the Lake Worth Lagoon (*aka* the Intracoastal Waterway). Thus the name Mar-a-Lago, which means "sea to lake" when translated from Spanish to English. Set back on A1A, it offers outstanding views and acres of manicured grounds that only hint of the opulence and beauty found beyond its stately wrought iron gates. Without a doubt, it is the crown jewel of Palm Beach Island.

Upon her death in 1973, the cereal heiress willed the residence to the US government, but high maintenance costs led the government to return the property to the Post family. In 1985, this storied South Florida palace was purchased by Donald Trump and continues to be a property of the Trump Organization. Trump and his first wife, Ivana, spent years renovating it.

When Donald expressed his intent to turn Mar-a-Lago into a world-class private club for people of means, it was met by opposition from the island's town council. Council members perceived the real estate mogul as being an ostentatious outsider. The brash New Yorker was certainly the antithesis of the "proper" upper-crust residents from old-guard families who made Palm Beach their winter home. I think they feared he might invite Jews or people of color into his club, if they could pay the hefty membership costs. Therefore, those in the island's inner circle of old money did not think well of him or of his club concept. Yet, Donald eventually won his battle and opened the Mar-a-Lago Club in 1995.

I wanted the Adler Network to be part of the team that would help him with his club's grand opening. After all, we knew public relations, we knew Palm Beach, and we knew luxury. I, however, did not know Donald Trump.

Nevertheless, I was confident that our agency was ideally suited for the job.

To tell this story, I need to take you back to the fall of 1993. Through my relationship with the Boca Raton Resort and Club's Premier Club, I had developed a friendship with Daniel Wielhouwer who was helping the Premier Club with its membership sales program. When I told Dan that I wanted to present a proposal to Donald Trump for an unforgettable grand opening that would attract Palm Beach society and other prospective club members to the magnificent mansion, he suggested that I speak with Dennis Hillier. Based in Boca Raton, Dennis specialized in real estate, land development, and hospitality industry law, with an emphasis on the design of club membership programs. Dan thought that Dennis could connect me with Donald Trump.

Dan had been correct. During our conversations with Dennis, he challenged the Adler Network to plan "the best social event Palm Beach society has ever seen" and then present our proposal to Donald. But first, we had to do our homework. I knew it was always best to have as much meat on the bone as possible before sitting down with any potential client, let alone someone as significant as Donald Trump.

Through Dennis, I was permitted access to Mar-a-Lago on numerous occasions. Each time I went there, I was in awe, not only of the beautiful surroundings and architecture, but also of the interior furnishings, down to every last detail.

My informative tour guide might have been the property caretaker, but to me he seemed more of a curator. Although I never knew the gentleman's official title, he had a wealth of facts that I eagerly soaked up and retained. Among them was that Marjorie Merriweather Post would sometimes invite houseguests to stay for a month at a time. Those guests would be served three meals a day—breakfast, lunch and dinner, and they never saw the same china, sterling, or crystal stemware. This mansion housed a thirty-day supply of three different place settings for each day. It was literally a treasure trove, and I (a zealous lover of antiques, fine china, and crystal) was both fascinated and overwhelmed. I returned again and again to find out more interesting stories about the rich history of the property and get to know the layout.

After I had the background information I needed about Mar-a-Lago, I gathered a team of top professionals and began working on a grand opening proposal for the new club. Event creator Bruce Sutka was among them. He was well known in Palm Beach and had terrific credentials, having once been married to a woman whose family was old guard. Bruce was full of fresh innovative ideas. He was incredibly talented and operated a design and production company that put on legendary cutting-edge parties and weddings for A-list residents and charitable organizations at venues such as the Flagler Museum and the Breakers. As a result, he knew the ins and outs and the who's who of Palm Beach better than we did. We were thrilled to work with him on this endeavor.

I can still remember the phone call that Owen and I made to Donald Trump in order to set up an appointment in New York to present our proposal. We had been working on the proposal for weeks, getting our ducks in a row, coming up with all of the details and determining every possible cost. Donald was on speaker phone with us during that call. Our staff was listening in as well, and I recall being embarrassed for them because the sound bites from his mouth were quite frequently four-letter words. I kid you not. Nevertheless, I wanted to orchestrate the Mar-a-Lago Club's grand opening. I set a date and time for us to meet with him in his office at Trump Tower.

Owen and I had pulled an all-nighter the night before we flew to New York, fine tuning and putting the finishing touches on our proposal. Arriving in New York on Sunday afternoon, we stayed at a very expensive chichi hotel. We only did this because Dennis Hillier was traveling with us, and he was booked there. My husband and I planned to meet with Donald early the next morning and then stay over a second night so we could enjoy the city and have some time to ourselves. Forget about seeing a Broadway show or going to the

Metropolitan Opera. We were looking forward to strolling along the avenues and eating hot dogs from a Sabrett cart vendor!

Before our scheduled meeting, Dennis mentioned that Donald was planning to marry his girl friend, Marla Maples, that evening.

Donald was on time for our meeting, just as we were. There were four of us seated around a table: Donald, a female assistant, Owen, and me. We sat there and went through our entire proposal with him. We had made him a copy so he could peruse our ideas as we talked about them. Our presentation reflected the grandeur and tradition of elegance of Mar-a-Lago. We believed there was only one way to introduce a private club housed in one of the most glamorous and recognized estates in the world, and that was with *style*. Furthermore, the rationale behind every aspect of the grand opening was based solely on creating the prestigious image of the Mar-a-Lago Club and the allure of becoming a member, which would generate the maximum return on each event expenditure.

After we had completed our presentation, he said, "This is the deal I'm going to make with you."

I was hanging onto my chair, expecting to become inflated. I could almost feel the top of my head touching the ceiling.

"I'm not going to pay you [the event planning, coordination, and public relations fee] because everyone will know that you are working for 'Donald Trump.' By using my name, you'll get every client you've ever wanted." He was dead serious.

My heart sank, and my spirits took a nose drive. My hopes were punctured. I looked toward Owen who was a very astute businessman with a lot of marketing savvy.

"Okay, we'll make a deal with *you*, Donald. We will put on the grand opening for the Mar-a-Lago Club and eat our fees *if* you promise that every property you develop in South Florida in the future will hire the Adler Network as its public relations firm," my husband said. This sounded fair to me since we would be relinquishing a $40,000 fee upfront. The remaining budget, totaling about $600,000 or higher with the optional items we had suggested, were "hard" event costs, which Donald would need to pay.

Then as if on cue, Donald's assistant announced, "Mr. Trump, you have a telephone call." Donald immediately left the room and was replaced by someone we considered to be a henchman. It was our impression that this guy was the one who would close the deal we had put on the table.

"I hope you realize what a great opportunity this is for you," he told us.

"We certainly do," I said. Owen nodded in agreement.

"But Mr. Trump is *not* going to make you any promises," the man announced. His tone was firm, as if this was the last word.

Owen and I had been willing to absorb our fee in exchange for Donald Trump's future Florida business. But it was now apparent to us that this wasn't going to happen. Meanwhile, Donald had our proposal in his possession, which was in essence a blueprint, so he could duplicate our grand opening concept, *if* he chose to do so. We were not protected. That was the mistake we continued to make through the years. We gave out too much information by putting *too* much meat on the bone. Consequently, any prospective client of ours had a full-blown plan on how to do something just like we would do it. In this case, we had outlined the exact menu items, the precise brands of fine wines and premium liquors (with quantities), and broken down equipment rentals to the last three-tiered silver pastry tray. We had presented all technical specifications in great detail and given the recommended numbers of doormen, runners, valet parking supervisors, attendants, and security officers. We even had suggested celebrity entertainment with specifics and costs. That was just the tip of the iceberg, or I should say "ice sculpture." Shame on us, I suppose. But when we made our presentations, they were so comprehensive that prospective clients were very impressed, and more often than not, they hired us.

After hearing the man's crushing words, I turned to Owen and said, "We need to leave." And we did just that.

Not only did I feel as if we had been dismissed and disrespected, but I honestly believed that our skill and capabilities had been invalidated. I had spent countless hours at Mar-a-Lago. Owen, I, and our team also had put in hours and hours in research and meetings to develop our proposal, only to have been met with what, in my opinion, was pompous posturing and bigger-than-life arrogance.

We hailed a taxi from Trump Tower to return to our fancy-schmancy hotel. En route, the cab driver misjudged the space he could drive though on a very narrow street, and a car coming from the opposite direction toward us ripped off the taxi's right-hand doors to the front and back seats! Although the cabby asked us to stick around to be witnesses for a police report, I didn't care about his taxi at that moment. I just wanted to get away from there.

Owen and I walked from wherever that location was to our hotel. The concierge greeted us warmly, "Hello. How are you today, Mr. and Mrs. Adler?"

"I want to get out of New York City," I said. "We're packing. We're leaving. Please get us a flight back to Fort Lauderdale *now*."

We gave up our additional night in the city and returned home instead.

Although we did not come to terms with Donald Trump over our proposal and were not involved in his club's grand opening, Owen and I returned to Mar-a-Lago many times for events for the Unicorn Children's Foundation and other charities that we worked with through the years. It had become more exciting for those organizations to hold their galas at Mar-a-Lago than at the Breakers or elsewhere in Palm Beach. The Mar-a-Lago venue was exceptional.

Sometimes Donald would attend those events. He was very gracious.

At that time, we couldn't possibly have known that Mar-a-Lago would turn out to be his "Winter White House!"

CHAPTER 14

Miami Design District

THE ADVANCEMENT OF REAL ESTATE development in the early to mid eighties in South Florida led to an expanding interior design industry, and the Adler Network was fortunate to have been involved in it. At the time, designers were centralized in the Miami Design District, located west of Biscayne Boulevard in the vicinity of North Fortieth Street, less than three miles from downtown. The area was open to the trade only and had an exciting cachet. Old warehouse space (in what historically has been known as the Buena Vista neighborhood) had been transformed into design studios, home furnishing showrooms, and art galleries. There also were a few restaurants. My favorite was David Harrison's Food among the Flowers with its cascading waterfalls, blossoming flowers, and enticing food presentations. I ate there often.

The early design industry in South Florida was mostly made up of gay men and women. They belonged to the American Institute of Interior Designers (AID) and the National Society of Interior Designers (NSID), which joined together to become the American Society of Interior Designers (ASID). I frequently referred to those groups as the "alphabet soup" of the design industry.

Members and associate members attended the meetings of those professional organizations. I did as well because some of the members were clients of ours. This, along with doing pro bono work for the Miami Design District itself, gave us name recognition and helped the Adler Network to grow its business.

There was a funny thing about those designers. They would socialize and network at meetings, but never discuss their clients. They feared that other designers might then try to steal their clients and make them their own.

There was, however, a lot of incredible local talent. Owen and I carried portfolios of our clients' professionally photographed interiors to New York and showed them to editors of publications there. We wanted to prove to them that South Florida wasn't all kitschy, with chartreuse walls, rattan, and tropical prints. In that respect, our agency was very much in the forefront of the design industry, showing the high-quality work that came out of this region.

Simultaneously, we were getting clients in the luxury real estate development field. Since real estate and design go hand in hand, this worked well for us. And that symbiotic relationship continued to work well for us for years to come. It also benefited many of our clients.

ASID put on annual black-tie fundraisers, which were always memorable. We helped with them, and I loved attending them. The gay male designers, in particular, had a great sense of style—a different sense of style. They were impeccably dressed and very elegant. So, in my eyes, those events were fashion shows as well.

One year I came up with an idea for an event themed "Gone with the Wind." Aside from the theme, the concept was to involve media personalities and challenge them about what they and other news reporters were implying: that gay designers were bringing HIV and AIDs to South Florida. While it was never directly stated that way, there were innuendos and broad-brush generalizations. The message conveyed was that if someone had HIV or AIDs, he was transmitting the virus and the disease; and every gay person who tested positive for HIV would die. This bothered us a lot. The gay design community wanted to change those negative overtones by educating the press, and I wanted to help them.

I approached co-anchors Ann Bishop and Dwight Lauderdale at the local ABC affiliate, WPLG Channel 10, and invited them to cochair the event. Ann was the first female broadcaster in a major market to co-anchor the early and late evening news. Dwight was the first African American television news anchor in South Florida. They were a great team with a large following.

They gave me a wishy-washy "We're not really sure about this," and "We don't know how the station will feel about this" type of response.

"I'll tell you what I'm doing to do," I countered. "I'm going to take out a full-page ad in the *Miami Herald* on my own dime and say that you didn't want to participate in our event. So take this information to the powers that be, and see what they want to do."

Ann and Dwight got back to me and said they'd serve as the cochairs.

I had not made an idle threat. I would have taken out that ad because I always worried about the underdog. I wanted a level playing field. I felt that everyone should be treated equally. I still do.

The event was held at Vizcaya, the historic Italian Renaissance-style villa and formal gardens built around 1916 as the winter home of industrialist James Deering. It could not have been a better venue. More than a thousand South Florida designers attended. They also had an opportunity to see the NAMES Project AIDs Memorial Quilt. I had reached out to the organization in San Francisco that had it in its possession and convinced them that it should be shown at Vizcaya during our event. Back then, the quilt was just in its infancy. It hadn't yet become the size of a football field—or larger. Nevertheless, it was a poignant visual memorial for people who had died from complications from AIDS. The hand-crafted volunteer effort was meant to heal those who had lost loved ones. It also was an educational tool to bring public awareness about the disease and inspire action to help prevent it.

It was not known, at that time, that this quilt would become the largest ongoing community art project in the world. According to the aidsquilt.org website, NAMES Project Foundation chapters have developed across the United States, and there are independent affiliates worldwide. Each has raised tremendous amounts of money to help stop the AIDS pandemic. In addition, the more than forty-eight thousand panels that make up the AIDS Memorial Quilt have been photographed for an enduring visual documentation.

Our goal for that event had been to educate media so that they would not continue to spread the fear factor about AIDS and South Florida's gay design community. I'm proud to say we achieved it.

Not long after, and unrelated to this, a female designer was mugged while walking along the Miami Design District. This led the city to put policemen on horseback to patrol the streets.

The district eventually succumbed to urban crime and decay. South Florida's sharp real estate downturn in 1989 contributed to its demise, as did the growing popularity of the relatively new DCOTA (Design Center of Americas) complex in neighboring Broward County. It wasn't until redevelopment of the Miami Design District began in the late 1990s and early 2000s that design studios, home furnishings shops, and art establishments again opened, starting a renaissance that could be compared to New York's SoHo a decade earlier.

Much like Miami's edgy art district of Wynwood, the Miami Design District's revitalization has been remarkable. Aside from offering high-end design services and fine items for the home, there are retailers like Cartier, Dior, Givenchy, Versace, and Louis Vuitton selling their luxury brands. And there are new restaurants galore. Consequently, local residents and jet-setting tourists are drawn to this renewed area. There is also a residential component—rental apartments and condos added into the mix, confirming the popular back-to-the-city New Urbanism trend.

CHAPTER 15

An International Design Destination

DCOTA

IT WAS DCOTA THAT TURNED South Florida into a major interior design destination. People no longer had to go to New York City or High Point, North Carolina, to shop for high-end furnishings. Home and office furniture, antiques, accessories, art, fabrics, and floor, window, and wall coverings were located within this multi-building design center in Dania (since renamed Dania Beach).

And we knew about it when it was only a vision.

I was making dinner at home one evening in 1983 when I received a call from a man who identified himself as Marvin Danto from Troy, Michigan. He asked if Owen and I could meet with him and his son the next morning at eight o'clock. I agreed, although I had never heard of him. There was no Internet access back then, so I couldn't simply Google his name.

I immediately placed a call to Lewis Goodkin, a real estate consultant who was a friend of mine, to see if he had ever heard of Marvin Danto. Not only had Lew heard of Marvin, but he also encouraged me to attend the meeting. Lew said that he had a client who owned the land that Marvin was bidding on in Dania.

The following morning, Owen and I met with Marvin and his son Jim at a Marriott Hotel in Fort Lauderdale where they literally picked our brains for two hours. During that conversation Marvin told us he had built the

Michigan Design Center in Troy. Now he had a desire to build one of the country's largest design centers in Dania. The location was ideal, minutes from the Fort Lauderdale/Hollywood International Airport, just off I-95 at Griffin Road and midway between Fort Lauderdale/Palm Beach and Hollywood/Miami.

Marvin broke ground on DCOTA that same year and opened the first phase in 1985. He hired Joan Kerns, a dynamite gal, to lease out the space. She eventually became DCOTA's executive vice president and a friend of mine.

Through the years, I tried to get Joan to retain the Adler Network as DCOTA's PR firm. But she spent most of the DCOTA marketing budget on advertising. There were no hard feelings. Furthermore, our agency already had ties to DCOTA. We were representing the Judith Norman, Kravet Fabrics, Nicoletti Italia, and D'Avila Collection showrooms, in addition to a wallpaper showroom in that location.

Marvin Danto's timing couldn't have been better. There was tremendous growth in real estate here because people were moving down from the Northeast Corridor, and they needed to furnish their new residences. Designers from South Florida, as well as from out of state, brought their clients to DCOTA and took them into the various showrooms to shop.

Judith Norman

I don't believe in coincidences, so when we had met Marvin and he told us about his plans for DCOTA, I said, "You know, Marvin, we represent Ted Fine, an interior designer here in South Florida. His son Mitchel is in medical school but he doesn't want to continue on. Instead, Mitchel wants to open a home furnishings showroom in the area." Ted was going to put up the money so Mitchel could do this.

As fate would have it, Mitchel Fine's Judith Norman became the *first* showroom at DCOTA, and it became an Adler Network client from the start. Since Mitchel was on the DCOTA Advisory Board, I attended meetings at DCOTA along with him. We met regularly with Joan and her staff. I came up with marketing ideas without ever being on DCOTA's payroll, just because

I represented Judith Norman and cared about its success. One of my suggestions was for DCOTA to host events for designers in the beautiful atrium areas. I even told them *who* to invite. It used to drive me crazy that people would drive along I-95, see the DCOTA sign, and never know what it stood for. On-site events would entice more designers to visit DCOTA. They'd bring their clients there, and DCOTA would become busier.

I also came up with a novel idea for Mitchel: Judith Norman should offer complimentary lunch daily for designers and the clients they brought into his showroom. He did just that, and it turned out to be a very popular tactic. The food was a small price to pay and could be written off as a business expense. We both knew, for example, that if a designer brought in a couple and they liked the furnishings, they would want to leave to "grab a bite to eat." They'd say, "Let us think about it. We'll be back." But we knew if those clients left, the chances were slim that they'd ever return. By meeting their basic need for sustenance, Mitchel's showroom usually succeeded in making the sale right then and there.

A funny story had to do with the Judith Norman showroom and the home furnishing editor and design critic Jo Werne. Jo wrote about home and décor for the *Miami Herald* for much of her thirty-eight-year career with that major daily newspaper. Designers and retailers yearned for her attention. To be mentioned in her articles almost sealed the deal for becoming a success. She was a tastemaker and a consumer advocate, informing readers about quality, value, and trends.

I had cultivated a very close working relationship with Jo. When Judith Norman opened at DCOTA, I persuaded her to go see the showroom and interview Mitchel. I had told Mitchel to expect Jo's phone call and to set up a meeting. He apparently didn't let any of his staff know about this.

Jo placed her first call to Judith Norman. When the receptionist answered, Jo announced, "I'm Jo Werne from the *Miami Herald*. I'd like to speak with Mitchel Fine."

The receptionist, who thought that Jo was either selling a subscription or advertising space, told her they weren't interested and hung up.

Jo tried a second time. "This is Jo Werne from the *Miami Herald* again."

Before she could continue, the same receptionist said, "We don't want to subscribe or advertise in your newspaper. And Mitchel Fine is *not* here!" Of course, he was. But the receptionist again abruptly hung up the phone. On *Jo Werne*!

Jo tried one last time, solely because of the relationship she and I had. In this case, three times wasn't a charm.

Ringing. "Hello, Judith Norman. Can I help you?" asked the receptionist.

"Please don't hang up. This is Jo Werne from the *Miami Herald*, and I need to speak with Mitchel Fine. It's important."

"I already told you that we aren't interested in the *Miami Herald*. We don't want the *Miami Herald*. We don't need the *Miami Herald*. And we don't even like the *Miami Herald*," said the annoyed receptionist to Jo. *Click.*

Jo called me and told me what had happened. Of course, I was terribly embarrassed.

"It's only because I like and respect you, Maxine, that I am calling you about this. If it wasn't for you, I wouldn't be interested in writing about this showroom anymore," she said.

"Jo, I am so sorry! I will tell Mitchel what happened, and I promise, he will call you."

She agreed to take his call.

When I called Mitchel and told him what had occurred, he was mortified.

"What should I do about my receptionist, Maxine?"

Not one to get someone fired, I joked, "Hit her with a wet noodle. But before you do, call Jo Werne *now*. Here is her number. Sincerely apologize and set up a meeting with her to come to Judith Norman. Then let me know when the meeting has been scheduled, and I'll be there with you."

Whenever possible, I always was present while my clients were being interviewed by the press. Though I sat quietly in the background, I was there to jump in and steer the conversation in the right direction if I felt help was required.

Mitchel did what I asked him to do, and it resulted in a wonderful article by the journalistic expert on interior design in South Florida. Only then did I breathe a sigh of relief.

As time went by, I remember Mitchel telling me that he didn't fear online competition when it arose. Businesses had just begun peddling their wares on the Internet.

"You have to sit in a chair to know it's comfortable. People want to see it, feel the fabric, and try it out," he said. I agreed with him. Perhaps that's why Judith Norman is still one of the busiest showrooms in DCOTA and also why Mitchel has since opened a Maitland-Smith showroom (which now carries other manufacturers' products too), a Judith Norman Outdoor Living showroom, and a Judith Norman Now showroom, which sells home furnishing items available now.

I continue to speak with Mitchel. We still talk about the times that I coordinated events for Judith Norman, and visiting designers and other guests thought that *I* was Judith Norman! The name Judith Norman was conceived from a combination of Mitchel's father's middle name "Norman" and his mother's middle name "Judith." No one named Judith Norman actually existed. Yet people would greet *me* with a "Hello, Judith" or "Hello, Mrs. Norman." I would smile and show them around the showroom. It was all in a day's work.

FLORIDA DESIGN MAGAZINE

In 1980 Jeff Lichtenstein and Neil Hoffman began publishing the *New Homes Guide* locally. It featured the new real estate developments in the region but did not focus on interior design.

When the *New Homes Guide* held a real estate show at the DCOTA building, *Florida Design* magazine was started as a guide book to the showrooms located there. Distributed at that show, it contained very little editorial content and had a tiny circulation. This was in the early nineties.

Shortly after, Jeff noticed that an annual home-and-design type of publication was being put out by the former *Miami Magazine*, owned by Sylvan Myer. After seeing that magazine, Jeff said, "If they were successful doing it, we should do it but quarterly."

Jeff came to the Adler Network to meet with Owen and me because he knew we were involved in the design industry. He explained what he wanted to do and asked for our thoughts. We loved his idea and felt that he had identified a void in the local market. We also knew we could help him by providing great photography and information about our design clients' projects.

Jeff had relocated to South Florida from Baltimore where his parents, Paul and Phyllis Lichtenstein, had owned a home furnishing showroom. It was obvious to us that Jeff understood business and the design field. In *Florida Design*, he saw a niche opportunity to promote high-end homes and condominiums in Florida in a similar way that *Architectural Digest* already was doing nationwide. But he wanted his magazine to reflect a subtropical style that differed from other parts of the country. He also was interested in showing readers the elements that pull a room together successfully.

So, after about a year, Jeff expanded and changed the editorial content in *Florida Design*. Then three years later, a large newsstand distribution through Time Warner was implemented. As the magazine grew, its content showcased fine furnishings, interior design, and architecture for projects in Florida, the Caribbean, and other tropical locations.

The magazine's masthead emulated that of *Architectural Digest*—the same black font against a white background. The format of *Florida Design* was also similar in nature. I'll never know how Jeff was able to pull that off! But he did, and his magazine will enter its twenty-seventh year in 2017.

From its early status as a fledgling guide book, *Florida Design* has grown to a whopping four hundred fifty pages. Because of its widespread international distribution, you can visit any major airport in the world today and are likely to find *Florida Design*. Consequently, the magazine's advertisers, as well as its featured designers, are provided with global exposure to help sell their home furnishing products and design services respectively.

Jeff proved to be an adept entrepreneur. To his credit, he also publishes two other glossy magazines: *Miami Home and Décor* and *Palm Beach the Island*.

Florida Design's first managing editor was Karen King (McCallum). She had once worked at the Adler Network. Jeff's mom Phyllis was a senior executive with the magazine. On many occasions, I drove Phyllis around South Florida with me to visit my clients' recent "installations." That's design-industry language for newly completed interior spaces. If Phyllis liked what she saw, then I worked with the designers to have the residences professionally photographed and submitted to *Florida Design*. I also arranged for the designers to be interviewed.

The magazine is truly a family affair. Jeff is the president and publisher; his wife Barbara is editor-in-chief; his dad Paul is the comptroller; and Phyllis still is involved as well.

I also want to mention Annette Galbo, the magazine's editorial coordinator. Annette is terrific, and she was my "go-to" person when I initially "pitched" the works of my Florida-based interior design clients to *Florida Design* with the hope that they would deem them publishable. They oftentimes did.

Everyone at *Florida Design* was a true professional to work with, and we even had some of our clients in the home furnishings and real estate development fields partner with this magazine for events through the years. One example follows.

HUMANITARIAN DESIGNER OF THE YEAR

In 1998, when the Adler Network was representing Boca Developers' new Townsend Place in downtown Boca Raton, we held an on-site event in order to attract hundreds of South Florida's top designers who had clients with the means to afford a condominium residence there.

But what exactly would make interior designers attend such an event? Recognition among their peers.

Although it wasn't an Oscar, Emmy, or Tony awards presentation, the idea for this event was the first-ever Humanitarian Designer of the Year competition. Likewise, a Lifetime Achievement award was given out during the "black tie optional" evening. Boca Developers' partners Brian Street and Jim Cohen were the hosts and sponsors, and *Florida Design* magazine and the International Sales Group (ISG) were participants. We selected a distinguished panel of judges that included Joan Kerns, executive vice president of

DCOTA; Jo Werne, the *Miami Herald*'s home furnishing editor; and Linda Corley Webb of WPBT/Channel 2, executive producer of the syndicated *Décor* show.

The judges had their work cut out for them, as many of the nominated individuals had made significant contributions to humanitarian causes. Designer Harvey Le Vine of R.H. Design Group in Miami Beach and Gloria Jean Blake were the stars of the night, winning the Humanitarian Designer of the Year award and the Lifetime Achievement award respectively. Gloria had been the editor of a national design publication in Manhattan before she moved to South Florida with her husband and daughter, Susan Preville. Gloria then cofounded and had been editor-in-chief of *Florida Designers Quarterly*, which thrived from 1977 into the eighties before ceasing publication. She is thought by many to have elevated South Florida's design industry from a cottage industry into one that competes nationally and internationally. Also, many of the designers in attendance attributed much of their success to Gloria's early encouragement and support. It was her dedication in the field that earned her the Lifetime Achievement honor on that evening.

We had given Boca Developers the idea of commissioning Gallery Bolae of Miami to create two sculptured crystal awards, one for each of the winners (yet to be named). Each piece was beautiful, but one was larger and a bit more impressive than the other. When wrapping each sculpture, we had faintly marked which recipient should receive each piece. The more substantial piece was to go to Gloria.

When Joan Kerns named Gloria a winner, she gave her the sculpture meant for Harvey. And Jeff Lichtenstein of *Florida Design* then gave Harvey the other one. There was nothing we could do about it. We were, however, glad that no one other than the Adler Network knew about this inadvertent faux pas.

The best laid plans sometimes do *go awry!*

CHAPTER 16

Stitched at the Hip

IN THE SUMMER OF 1995, Judy Goldstein was hired by the Jewish Federation of Fort Lauderdale, which was merging with the Jewish Federation of Hollywood. The new entity was initially called the Jewish Federations of Broward County. (Later the "s" in "Federations" was dropped.) Someone had created a new position for Judy as assistant communications director after she had served voluntarily on the Public Relations committee at the Fort Lauderdale Federation location a year earlier. That same woman became Judy's boss when she was hired. Judy worked with a great team, writing press releases and other materials, generating publicity, and editing several Federation publications. She also worked at their fundraising events.

At first, I was sure that this would be my dream job. The Jewish Federation was a wonderful organization, and I felt that—in some small way—I was contributing to the local community as well as helping Jews abroad. But within six months, I realized that I had the boss from hell. She was disrespectful of my time and took advantage of me in ways I believed were unacceptable.

Like me, over the years Judy had developed a close working relationship with Kevin Murphy, the journalist in charge of the *Sun-Sentinel*'s Real Estate section. It was the largest section of its kind in the country, filled with information about new homes, condominiums, townhomes, and communities throughout South Florida and the Treasure Coast. If anyone was seeking a home in the region, they'd read that section first. Kevin also put together the Jewish Federation's *Shalom* newspaper; Judy was the managing editor. The two of them met every Sunday night to work on the layout of that weekly newspaper, which was tucked inside of the *Sun-Sentinel*. When Judy became disenchanted with her job, she mentioned it to Kevin. He told her he knew of a PR firm in Fort Lauderdale that had been looking for an account supervisor and writer for a very long time.

"They do good work. Call Maxine Adler," he said. He then gave me the phone number of the Adler Network. During my lunch break at the Jewish Federation, I called Maxine, who I was told was on another call. Yet Maxine picked up the phone to speak to me. I liked that right away. We talked briefly, and I told her I'd like to interview for the position at the Adler Network, but that I couldn't do it during working hours. She suggested that I come in for an interview after work that same week.

When Judy arrived at our office in early February 1996, I welcomed her and we sat down together. As soon as I opened her portfolio, I saw that it was brimming with bylined feature stories that she had written as a contributing writer to many local lifestyle magazines and newspapers. I immediately took note of this because bylines were the real deal in the PR industry. They meant that a person could write—and write well in order to get published. She also showed me a large sampling of publicity clips, which she had garnered on behalf of clients she represented while employed elsewhere. In her current position at the Jewish Federation, one of her responsibilities included being the managing editor of the *Shalom* newspaper (produced by the *Sun-Sentinel*) and the *Jewish Herald* (produced by the *Miami Herald*). Judy was a prolific writer, and I was impressed. Anyone would have been.

As I just said, I found it reassuring to see an abundance of articles that carried Judy's byline. Years earlier, I had interviewed a gal who showed me copies of two articles with her name on them. She said that she had a lot more samples at home but hadn't brought them along. I soon doubted that they ever existed because after I hired her and asked her to write a simple press release, she couldn't even write a simple declarative sentence! She must have had an excellent editor who made her look good. Or maybe this new employee had "whited out" the real author's name and replaced it with her own name on the articles she had shown me. She didn't last the week.

Judy's experience covered a wide range of industries, and the topics she had written about were diverse. I especially noted the content that related to the real estate and design industries because that had become the Adler Network's specialty. I kept looking at her work, and when I saw an article she had penned for *Gold Coast* magazine in the early eighties, I was delighted. It addressed the development that was taking place out west. At that time, "west" was at Powerline Road, in the Fort Lauderdale/Pompano Beach areas. She had written about Palm-Aire Country Club and the residences offered there. How great was this? My agency was *currently* representing Palm-Aire Country Club in order to promote new memberships and reinforce the value of resales in the community.

When perusing the articles she had written after interviewing a number of celebrities, I came across one about a performer I had booked for a Roscioli golf event at Bonaventure Resort in Fort Lauderdale. (This was Bobby Rydell, and Judy and Bobby maintain a friendship to this day, after thirty years.) Likewise, Judy had been involved in a client tie-in with a Miss Universe Contest; I had done a client tie-in with a Miss America Contest at about the same time. Something clicked.

When she spoke to me about her personal life, something clicked again. Judy was a divorced woman, with two adult children, who supported herself; I thought she must be a hard worker. I also thought she was looking for the long game. Before her brief stint with Jewish Federation, she had put in a decade heading up the PR division for a local ad agency. She demonstrated longevity and loyalty.

At the time, Judy lived in Jacaranda Lakes in Plantation like Owen and I did. After Judy told me that her mom's name was Honey, I told her that my daughter-in-law was called Honey. Also, Owen never addressed me as Maxine. I was always his "honey." This was becoming eerier every minute— this connection I felt. Somehow I knew it was *beshert* (meant to be). I immediately sent Judy into Owen's office to talk about compensation and benefits.

I was impressed from the minute I opened the door to the Adler Network. The office, located in the Cypress Creek/I-95 area, was drop-dead gorgeous. I could see that the agency had wonderful credentials and notable clients. Why hadn't I heard of this company before? Because I hadn't had to search for a job in more than a decade. Before I joined the Jewish Federation, I had started the PR division for an ad agency in Pompano Beach, and stayed there for ten years before moving on. I was a loyalist, until I chose to leave a job, as I now wanted to do.

My meeting with Maxine had been great, and I thought that she liked me. We seemed to have "gelled." There was a like-mindedness. Then, after chatting with Owen Adler for a while and feeling comfortable, we talked money.

"What's your salary requirement?" he asked. I took a deep breath, smiled confidently, and stated "Thirty-six thousand dollars." This was a little more than I was currently earning at the Jewish Federation and a decent chunk of change for a PR executive in Florida back in 1996. Owen said that he and Maxine would arrive at a decision and let me know if I got the job. I'd get a call the next day.

I drove home, ate a bite, and then showered. The phone rang as I was drying myself off. When I answered, Owen was on the other end offering me the position of account supervisor and writer. I accepted while reprimanding myself. I should have asked for more money! Although I didn't, I was rewarded with a series of raises in a very short period of time, which continued over the years of my employment at the Adler Network. Furthermore, I was quickly promoted to the position of vice president of the agency.

Judy joined us, two other account supervisors, a graphic artist, and a receptionist, two weeks later after she had left her job at the Jewish Federation.

As I mentioned earlier, we were a small firm that was big on results. We always had a network of support around us (freelancers and vendors), if we needed them. With Judy now on our team, the business grew substantially. She was a work horse like I was.

In 2003 the *South Florida Business Journal* ranked the Adler Network, with a net PR fee income of $2.2 million annually, as the sixth largest PR firm in the South Florida region. And we earned that ranking with only eight employees. By comparison, the number five and seven slots had fifteen and twenty-three employees respectively!

Maxine told me if she could find two Judy clones, she would hire them. It never happened. I was flattered but disappointed. I would have settled for just one clone! The glamour of public relations was becoming outweighed by my workload, which was getting heavier and more stressful by the minute. Was I a glutton for punishment, or did I thrive because of the work I was doing? The latter is more likely.

From the start of my relationship with Judy, it became a love-in. We were simpatico. We thought the exact same thing at the same time. I would begin a sentence, and she would finish it; and vice versa. We became stitched at the hip. Furthermore, people frequently mistook us for sisters. We both were thin and had dark hair. Sometimes they referred to Judy as "Judy Adler." She might as well have had our last name; she became a part of our family on a personal level too.

Judy had an exemplary work ethic, which she said she had learned from her dad.

My father always said to me, "If you're going to do something, do it the best way you can." So I pushed myself to become a perfectionist.

Although my mom didn't work, she was a perfectionist at home. I remember making my bed when I was a kid. She'd make it over again. If the sofa had a wrinkle in it, she would immediately smooth it out. And Mom never had a hair out of place, thanks to half a bottle of Aqua Net. I know I inherited some of those traits, but I did allow my daughters to make their own beds, without me making them over! I think I've mellowed a lot over time.

Judy played a big role in decisions about the agency—how to improve it, whom to hire, and so on. She was extremely well organized, gave meticulous attention to every last detail, and was a stickler for accuracy. As a matter of fact, a few of our clients asked her to proofread everything that their ad agencies produced before the materials went to a printer or a publication.

I couldn't always see my own mistakes, but I could spot someone else's a mile away.

Whenever we needed to hire a new employee, Judy and I set aside a Saturday, from nine to five o'clock, and scheduled candidates for interviews every hour. She screened each person and wrote down some of her thoughts in the margin of that person's resumé before sending them in to see me. After a day of interviews, we selected the best individual for the position and invited him or her back to the office that week to meet with Owen to discuss the "back of the house." This worked for us, with only a couple of exceptions.

One time, a new receptionist arrived to start working for us. Judy directed her to sit in our conference room to wait for me. I came parading by a few minutes later and Judy grabbed me, pulling me aside.

"I don't know who that girl is. Do you?" I asked Maxine because she certainly did not look like anyone we had interviewed or hired.

"I never saw her before in my life!" Maxine told me. "Let's get Owen."

When Owen peeked into the conference room to say hello, he quickly excused himself and joined Maxine and me in another part of the office.

"It sure beats me. I don't know who she is either!"

Apparently this girl had completely changed her appearance for the first day on the job at the Adler Network. It didn't matter; her clerical skills did not match her resumé. She was not at all prepared for the fast pace of PR, and she subsequently quit.

Another memorable receptionist had come to us from the design industry. Her mannerisms and the way she dressed for her interview had been very professional. But soon after we hired her, she began arriving at our office wearing the same clothes from the day before, and her hair was disheveled. She also looked drowsy. Once she told us her car had been stolen from our office parking lot. Another time, Judy saw her being pulled over on the side of the road by police officers. Too much late-night partying—or something else—eventually cost her the job.

Judy and I were completely engrossed in everything we did. We always drove together to client meetings and events. Sometimes she would park and leave her car at a designated location, and I would pick her up. On far too many occasions, we'd be so energized and engaged in conversation on the drive back that I'd forget to drop her off to get her car. Usually we'd pass by multiple exits before we realized what had happened. Or we'd arrive at the office and then have to drive back in the direction we had just come from in order to retrieve her car. On one occasion, we missed an exit, got onto Alligator Alley, and ended up at the Miccosukee Indian Reservation!

Unless you have ever experienced this "specialness" with another person, it may be difficult to comprehend. To this day, Judy is one of the only persons I can reminisce with. We meet occasionally for lunch or dinner and become recharged all over again by reliving these—and countless other—stories.

More often than not, we are in tears from laughing. Although we are no longer stitched at the hip, it often feels that way.

In the early nineties, my cousin Barbara coaxed me to go with her to see a psychic. When I did, I was told that I would have a very important and long-lasting relationship with someone whose name started with the letter M. Because I was divorced, I always equated "relationship" to romance. A few years later, I dated someone named Mark, but it lasted only a few months. Plus, while we were dating, I knew he wouldn't be the M. It wasn't until I was employed at the Adler Network for nearly a decade that I remembered this incident. Little did I know back then, when I had met with that psychic, that the M would be "Maxine."

Also, I certainly didn't know that the psychic, Rose Marks of Fort Lauderdale, would be imprisoned years later for defrauding clients!

CHAPTER 17

A Forte for Fashion

ANOTHER COMMON THREAD INTERWOVE ITS way into the closely knit Adler-Goldstein relationship, which further strengthened our connection. It was fashion.

Following World War II, fashion had experienced a rebirth and hats became an important part of a well-dressed woman's wardrobe. My mother and father, Faye and Herman Schwartz, were in the millinery business. They owned several ladies' hat shops in northern New Jersey during the late forties, fifties, and sixties.

Maxine's, located in Passaic, opened on the day I was born. My parents named this store after me, and it quickly became known as a place for stylish women to buy their hats. It was the most "high end" of all my parents' stores; Maxine's also sold name brand handbags such as Judith Leiber and Rosenfeld. The hats were custom designed and made on the premises by a talented millinery designer, Joey Riché, and numerous seamstresses. Joey was a bit rough around the edges and used language that matched his demeanor. The ladies didn't seem to mind, but my mother did. (After Maxine's eventually closed down, Joey went to work at the Concord Resort Hotel in New York opening for the Borscht-Belt comedians and crooners who headlined there during the heydays of the Catskills.)

My mother was a fashion aficionado who believed in building an outfit from the top down; a hat began one's attire. After her customers had their custom hat in hand, she would then suggest the best clothing styles, colors and accessories to accompany it. Conversely, if they brought in a dress or suit, she would suggest the best color and look for a hat, and they'd have one made at Maxine's.

My parents' other hat stores carried less expensive merchandise, including handbags and costume jewelry, at varying price points. Each store had a different name. At one time or another, before I was married, I helped out at every one of them.

Always beautifully groomed and making a stunning appearance, my mom was singled out as being among America's best-dressed women on behalf of the millinery industry. The annual events were elegant evening affairs held at the Waldorf Astoria in Manhattan. She received this award on multiple occasions in the fifties. It was presented by the fashionable Dorothy Kilgallen, the popular gossip columnist, journalist, and panelist on the television game show *What's My Line*. Many of the honorees were celebrities and socialites, so it was quite a distinction for my mom to receive since she was neither.

They say that the apple doesn't fall far from the tree. In my case, I guess it didn't. In 1990, I was recognized as the Region's Most Stylish Female Executive by *South Florida Magazine* and featured in its May issue. My counterpart was WPLG-Channel 10 anchor Dwight Lauderdale, who was chosen as the Region's Most Stylish Male Executive. I could not have been in better company. I knew Dwight from the time he had cochaired the ASID designer event at Vizcaya.

The day that we were to be photographed by *South Florida Magazine* for the article, Dwight and I had to change our clothes, together, inside of a small closet. Owen and Dwight's delightful wife were waiting for us on the other side of the door. There was a lot of trust. And Dwight was a true gentleman.

To get back on track, Judy's fashion story also became relevant when we worked together. Like me, she was the daughter of a retailer. Her father, Henry Liff, had owned a chain of hard-and-soft goods stores in Cleveland, Ohio, where she grew up. When she was a child, her parents sometimes took her with them on business trips to New York. There they visited children's clothing manufacturers'

showrooms on Seventh Avenue. Her dad chose dresses for her right off the rack. In addition, he frequently bought closeouts (off season) girls' and ladies' fashions. They were stored in the Liffs' basement, first in their home in Shaker Heights and later in their home in Beachwood. Judy and her mom would get first pick before her dad sold the remaining merchandise to other family members and friends. I suspect that Judy and her mother were always well dressed.

At sixteen, Judy took a summer job as an executive trainee at the May Company in Cleveland. She also was selected to be on the Bonwit Teller Teen Board along with girls from other area high schools. They modeled in the downtown store. That's when she decided, initially, to pursue a career in fashion.

She studied fashion and journalism for several years at Ohio State University, then transferred and graduated from the Tobé-Coburn School on Madison Avenue in New York City. At that time, the elite college only accepted women and was solely for fashion careers. As the first school in the nation to specialize in both fashion merchandising and promotion, it was highly regarded in the industry.

While attending classes and taking field trips, we were always recognized as "Tobé-Coburn girls." The stringent dress code called for dresses or suits with jackets, skirts and blouses, stockings, hats, and gloves. This was in the late sixties, before it became acceptable for women to wear pantsuits—and ditch the hat and gloves.

Judy's first work-study period was as an assistant buyer at Macy's Herald Square, where she earned $100 per week. She was given a budget of $70,000, a significant amount of money back then and told to purchase children's gloves on Seventh Avenue. Then after taking an ad writing course at Tobé-Coburn, she was assigned as a fashion copywriter at advertising agency giant J. Walter Thompson.

I was in heaven. That's where I received validation, and it was also when I set my sights on becoming a professional writer. And I decided that my writing didn't necessarily have to be about fashion.

After graduating from Tobé-Coburn at a ceremony and luncheon held at the Waldorf Astoria, Judy moved to South Florida to live with her parents, although she would have preferred remaining in New York. They had relocated from Cleveland to Hollywood, Florida, a year before. Upon her arrival, she turned down a retailing job with Saks Fifth Avenue in Miami Beach. Instead, she worked as a receptionist for the developer of the Alden House, a new apartment complex on Collins Avenue, not far from where she lived.

It was the first time I had ever used an electric typewriter. When I broke it after two days, I was so embarrassed that I quit. Soon I was hired as an ad copywriter for a North Miami–based agency specializing in hospitality and travel industry clientele. I wrote brochures for the popular "theme" resorts along motel strip in Sunny Isles Beach (i.e., the Sahara, the Desert Inn) and hotels in Miami Beach (i.e., the Deauville, the Carillon) as well as brochures for Caesar's Palace in Las Vegas, and ads for the new Circus Circus Casino, which was opening there. By then, I had become accustomed to using an electric typewriter! And several decades later, many of those Sunny Isles Beach "theme" motels were replaced by soaring high-rise condominiums.

As you might have guessed, people didn't yet own personal computers.

In the late sixties, Judy's dad and brother, Henry and Howard Liff, opened the first discount retail menswear operation in South Florida: Merchandise Liquidators in Hallandale (now called Hallandale Beach). They soon welcomed Howard's college friend Ed Gottlieb as a third partner.

The name "Merchandise Liquidators" was somewhat misleading because the store offered first-quality designer brands for a lot less than department stores did. No seconds or off-season goods. They worked on high volume and low profit. The formula worked.

The store initially grew its reputation by selling Nehru shirts and jackets in the late sixties and polyester Nik-Nik and Huck-a-Poo shirts during the seventies. (Those gaudy shirts were a favorite at disco clubs and worn by non-dancers too. They were quite the rage.) In the eighties, when Members Only jackets were ubiquitous, Merchandise Liquidators discounted the price and literally sold thousands of them to both men and women. The store also carried a full range of other menswear items, from ties to tuxedos. It was a common occurrence to see Rolls Royces and Bentleys in the parking lot. Even wealthy consumers were interested in saving money.

Other store locations opened. In Lauderdale Lakes, Morty Gaswirth became a minority partner and was in charge of the women's division. A Liff family cousin, Jeffrey Robbins, became a minority partner when Merchandise Liquidators later opened in Boca Raton.

Judy oftentimes wrote copy for Merchandise Liquidators' print ads and radio commercials. She didn't, however, go into the family business. She got married and had babies instead.

The first freelance feature article she wrote and sold was a multipage fashion feature in *Broward Life* magazine in 1980. It became a cover story entitled "The Jeaning of America" and was about the developing trend of "designer" jeans. *It showed a beautiful blonde on the cover wearing cowgirl attire from Teepee Western Wear in Hollywood. The inside pages of this fashion spread had other models wearing designer jeans with complementary clothing from Saks Fifth Avenue and Jordan Marsh at the Galleria Mall in Fort Lauderdale. I was so excited and proud that I bought fifty copies of that magazine and gave them away to my friends and relatives!*

When Judy re-entered the work force following her divorce, one of her jobs in the late seventies and early eighties was as an assistant editor, feature writer, and fashion columnist for the South Florida Newspaper Network owned by the *Sun-Sentinel*. This was the previous incarnation of what is now known as Forum Publishing (the *Hi-Riser, Eastsider, Jewish Journal, Boca Raton Forum, Delray Beach Forum*, and numerous other community newspapers).

I can still remember banging out copy on a very old manual Olivetti typewriter (it was a real relic) and proofreading the text on boards called "flats." I loved that job and loved the people whom I worked with, including a gorgeous Paul Newman look-alike who was thought to be gay. I didn't believe it until we were supposed to get together one evening. He cancelled and went to see the disco group, the Village People, instead. Ouch!

I doubt it was a coincidence that Judy's college graduation was held at the Waldorf Astoria in New York (where my mother had been honored many times), or that one of her family's menswear stores was located on Northwest Nineteenth Street in Lauderdale Lakes, a few bays away from our Bagel-O's business.

It was also uncanny that on many occasions, without having consulted one another, Judy and I dressed alike in some way or another, whether it was wearing all black, black-and-white stripes, or an animal print blouse.

One time we looked like the Doublemint Twins. We had an appointment with Leonard Woolfson and Cory King at their LenCor International Properties office in Miami Beach, and Judy and I were each wearing a winter-white pant-suit, black turtleneck top, and black suede half boots. We assured our clients that this duplication had been entirely unintentional. It truly was. Maxine and I were simply on the same wavelength. We still are. We could shop in each other's closet!

Our shared interest and involvement in fashion was a nexus that benefited many of our luxury real estate clients at the Adler Network. Quite often, we partnered with luxury fashion brands and fashion retailers in cross-promotional events. We also did this with luxury jewelers and luxury auto dealers because the market for new high-end real estate and these brands was the same. It was a win-win for everyone. And the guests liked those events. They enjoyed the eye candy.

In addition to the Emilio Pucci fashion show during the grand opening of the Esplanade in Palm Beach in 1980, our agency held fashion events for clients with Bloomingdale's and Saks Fifth Avenue in Boca Raton, Zola Keller in Fort Lauderdale, and other retailers in later years. Here are my favorite fashion events.

ELSA KLENSCH "STYLE"

In the late nineties, Judy and I were at a big marketing powwow at Boca Developers' office. Partners Jim Cohen and Brian Street had already built the Aragon condominium along the beach in Boca Raton, and they had just completed the first tower at Townsend Place in the downtown area across from the "Pink Plaza" (Royal Palm Plaza). Plans also were in the works for Mizner Grand overlooking Lake Boca Raton.

The subject of that particular meeting was to discuss an event at Townsend Place. Because this condo project had a beautiful, sprawling pool deck overlooking the Boca Raton Resort and Club's golf course, Maxine suggested an outdoor event for women.

"After all, women are big decision makers when it comes to where they and their husbands live," she told the group. The same thing is true if the husband has a mistress, she thought but didn't say.

That's when the idea of having a fashion show and luncheon took root.

That would not be a problem. What became a problem was Brian telling Maxine to bring in a celebrity for the event, and Maxine's response.

"I can get you Elsa Klensch," said Maxine with conviction. Elsa Klensch was an internationally recognized brand on CNN. As the cable network's fashion and design journalist, she had her own show, Style with Elsa Klensch. *No, Maxine did* not *know her.*

We were given the responsibility of conceiving the event, one in which Elsa Klensch would be the draw. The meeting ended.

On the way to the car, I asked Maxine, "Are you certifiably nuts? Why do you think you can get Elsa Klensch to come to Townsend Place? CNN will never permit her to endorse a product, let alone a luxury condominium!" I was the worrier between the two of us. Or if Maxine worried, she never showed it.

Maxine agreed that she didn't know how or if she could make this happen. But given the challenge, she surely would try.

I contacted the publicist for CNN, only to have her confirm what Judy had already told me.

"But what if we can come up with a 'hook'?" I asked the publicist.

"We will consider it, but we can't promise."

After brainstorming, Maxine reached out to Marta Batmasian, a commercial developer in town who also was involved with the Boca Raton Symphonic Pops. Not knowing Maxine or me, Marta still graciously agreed to a meeting with us. The rest became history and the event, chaired by Marta, was a very big one for Boca Raton.

The "hook" we created was multi-fold. First, this was Elsa's first appearance in Palm Beach County. Second, Symphonic Pops' Maestro Crafton Beck named the Australian-born journalist and show host an Honorary Conductor; and third, Elsa signed her book, *Style* (published in 1995), for guests at the end of the event. Each guest was given a complimentary book since we had arranged for Boca Developers to purchase copies of the book in advance. Working with Marta and her devoted volunteers, we held a beautiful luncheon, which included al fresco dining, informal modeling from several local retail shops, and a discussion about style and fashion by Elsa. The event was filled to capacity, and we were able to take guests on a tour of the property's first nine-story condo tower. Plus, the resulting publicity significantly increased awareness of Townsend Place. Our objective had been to make the connections between style, a luxurious life, and the cultural arts—with Boca Raton as the centerpiece. We succeeded.

From that time on, Maxine was my hero and probably the hero of many of the fashionable ladies and art patrons in Boca Raton! Maxine was also smart. That's why she also exposed Elsa to the very high-end oceanfront condominium, the Aragon. She arranged for Elsa to spend the night in a model residence there instead of in a hotel.

Postscript: We brought Elsa Klensch back to Boca Raton in 2004. She had left CNN and had written another book. This one was fiction, about the fashion industry she knew so well—*Live at 10:00, Dead at 10:15*, published that same year. We held a book signing event for her at Robb & Stucky's Mizner Park retail showroom. Robb & Stucky was our client.

ART OF FASHION

In 2003, in what had been unprecedented at the time, Neiman Marcus Bal Harbour closed its store for an entire evening so that our client WCI Communities could host a private invitation-only cocktail reception and high-energy runway fashion show. We planned this event, which was designed to promote WCI's new One Bal Harbour, a new residential and hotel condominium that was going to be built at the northernmost end of the Village of Bal Harbour directly overlooking the Atlantic Ocean and bordering Bakers Haulover Inlet. The Harbour House North rental apartment building was still on the site, but would eventually be demolished. So we had to hold this event close by yet off site. Neiman Marcus was the ideal venue.

The Dallas team from Neiman Marcus traveled to Bal Harbour to create the show environment. Clothing racks were relocated to make way for the podium and microphone, runway, chairs, and other essentials that included a beautiful backdrop with the WCI logo. When all was said and done, it looked like a fashion show that could have been held in Paris or Milan. It was a night of high drama and visual feasts, featuring the striking fashions worn by professional models. A sumptuous presentation of food from a local restaurant followed the show.

We had invited area VIPs, One Bal Harbour reservation holders, and prospective buyers (some of whom were the retailer's best customers). Cameras belonging to the fashion press captured the moves of female and male models wearing everything from designer jeans to evening attire. Featured fashion houses were Versace, Gucci, Roberto Cavalli, Marc Jacobs, Ralph Lauren, Pucci, St. John, YSL, Dolce and Gabbana, and Badgley Mischka.

What had been our rationale for this event? The Village of Bal Harbour was synonymous with high-end fashion, and WCI's real estate development would be located just blocks north of the Bal Harbour Shops, which was a global fashion designation. We felt that this unique tie-in with a preeminent retailer such as Neiman Marcus would reflect the sophistication of future One Bal Harbour residents. They were well educated, well traveled, well heeled, and well *dressed*.

The cooperation of Boris Milgrim, Neiman Marcus Bal Harbour's vice president and general manager, also was a way for this retailer to welcome future residents of the new condominium hotel to the neighborhood.

AN EVENING OF TIMELESS ELEGANCE

Although it wasn't a fashion show per se, our grand opening event for the Related Group of Florida's Las Olas Beach Club condominium in Fort Lauderdale in 2004 showcased a half-dozen professional models dressed in matching black evening gowns and sleek black-haired "bob" wigs. They were also decked out in vintage furs and jewels.

These glamorous models strolled among the guests, taking them back to the thirties era when the original building, the Lauderdale Beach Hotel, had enjoyed its heyday. Developer Jorge Perez's new property would consist of a portion of the historical structure, preserved and restored to its Art Deco appearance. It would house modern condo residences adjacent to a new twenty-nine-story condo tower.

We honored the Art Deco heritage of the site in "Old Hollywood" style, replete with velvet-roped stanchions and pin-striped paparazzi (who were actors) at the oceanfront Welcome Center. From there, guests entered a courtyard that had been transformed into an open-air club where oysters Rockefeller, steak Diane, shrimp, and caviar were served. Before the evening ended, a red-coated elevator valet attendant took guests to a sixth-floor Sky Bar, where they took in the views from the oceanfront terraces while sipping martinis and listening to smooth jazz.

Soon after, The Related Group incorporated photos of some of those "bobbed" models in their promotional campaign for the Las Olas Beach Club. They wanted to be consistent with the overall image we had created for the project.

CELEBRATION OF STYLE

The iconic fifty-three-unit ocean-to-Intracoastal condominium building One Thousand Ocean was located on the grounds of the Boca Raton Resort and Club's Boca Beach Club at the Boca Raton Inlet. Because this modern, nautilus-shaped, concrete, steel and glass structure epitomized "style," we celebrated that style with an evening fashion event.

We held it in One Thousand Ocean's largest penthouse, which had been turned into an event venue for occasions such as this one by Jamie Telchin, president of development for LXR Luxury Resorts. (An LXR affiliate developed this project.) He had help from marketing consultant Candace Jorrisma. The "raw" interior space had no interior walls and the voluminous ceiling was unfinished. It had been draped with white sheer curtains, and white carpeting had been installed. There was a bar, seating areas with white sofas and ottomans, and professional lighting. What made this space truly awesome was its size and views: approximately eight thousand seven hundred square feet of air-conditioned space and an additional four thousand five hundred square feet of terraces overlooking both the ocean and the Intracoastal Waterway. No one questioned its $15 million price tag. This penthouse would continue to be used for many other One Thousand Ocean events until it was sold.

We brought in Saks Fifth Avenue from the Town Center at Boca Raton as a partner, and the high-end retailer previewed the Holiday 2010 Couture Collection of Craig Signer.

Maxine was very familiar with this Bay Harbor Islands-based fashion designer because he had made special-occasion gowns for her for many years.

The show was fabulous, as were Craig's fashions. It culminated with a model wearing a wedding gown, followed by a final parade of models in stunning evening gowns.

On that same evening, Roberto Coin displayed showpiece jewels. Cocktails, great food, and a tour of One Thousand Ocean's furnished model residences made this event even more enjoyable for One Thousand Ocean buyers and prospective buyers. Also, Saks Fifth Avenue had invited its top Boca Raton customers, who probably could afford to purchase a residence in the building.

As with all Adler Network events, we weren't just filling space. The guests were qualified buyers.

FASHION COVER STORY

For its 2010 "Fall Fashions" cover story, Kevin Kaminski, the editor of *Boca Raton Magazine,* reached out to us to see if One Thousand Ocean would agree to become the backdrop for a multipage photo shoot. Of course, the developer of One Thousand Ocean would agree, and it wouldn't cost him a dime.

Judy and I coordinated everything with the magazine's team, and the resulting fashion spread had chic models posed in ways that showcased the magnificent ocean and Intracoastal views from the building.

Because *Boca Raton Magazine* was the city's premier city magazine, we had a very happy client. Plus, the ten pages of free publicity helped generate more traffic to the building.

FASHIONABLY PHILANTHROPIC

While doing pro bono work for the South Palm Beach County chapter of the National Parkinson's Foundation (NPF) in 2013, we held a "Fashionably Philanthropic" cocktail reception and runway fashion show that raised $40,000 for this worthy organization. The event was staged in One Thousand Ocean's last available penthouse. Although it was smaller in size than the largest penthouse, it was nevertheless very spacious and worked well.

Style aficionado Etoile Volin from the retail store Etoile in east Boca Raton constructed the runway and provided the fashions and the models—models such as local socialites Christian Lynn, Jan Savarick, and eight others. It was wonderful to see these ladies relaxed and rehearsing before the event, wearing only long Etoile T-shirts. No skirts, pants, shorts, or shoes. These gals were completely down to earth.

Stu Perlin, the charity chapter's executive director, brought in board members and other volunteers to help. One Thousand Ocean's developer gladly provided the venue, catering and valet parking. There also was an impressive display of sparkling gems from Manhattan-based Jeri Cohen Fine Jewelry, as well as limited-edition Louis Vuitton handbags from Lauren Schachter's Palm Beach Closet. Alpine Jaguar displayed two new motor cars near the building's grand entrance. All of these components gave the soirée even further panache from start to finish.

Best of all, aside from attracting new prospective buyers to One Thousand Ocean, the nonprofit NPF benefited from our efforts. The money raised that night went toward continuing the chapter's support groups for both patients and caregivers. It also perpetuated exercise and wellness classes for patients of Parkinson's disease.

CHAPTER 18

Doing Things Differently

BRIAN STREET, A TRANSPLANTED NATIVE of South Africa, met Jim Cohen through their respective children in the early nineties. Brian was an entrepreneur who had served in the military in South Africa and Israel. Jim was a resort developer and venture capitalist.

Both men enjoyed doing things differently and had something unique in common. Before they were ever introduced to one other and entered into a business relationship, each had taken a year off with their family to sail around the world. When their children returned to school in Boca Raton, they found out about the other family's travels. They were determined that their parents should meet. They did.

It has been said that Brian and Jim started their company on a handshake in 1992. The Adler Network worked with these partners when the firm was known initially as 2500 Developers based out of Boca Raton. A few years later, their luxury condominium development firm changed its name to Boca Developers and relocated its headquarters to Deerfield Beach. Representing them for approximately five years was an interesting journey for my agency.

Brian and Jim's first project was built on one of the last pieces of oceanfront land of any significance in Boca Raton. This was the Aragon, a trio of towers featuring a total of forty-six condominium residences. Because several buyers purchased two units, the building ended up having just forty-one owners. The low-density structure (which "hides" its three towers inside of a single facade) resembles a cruise ship with wide cantilevered terraces. It was purposefully designed so that each residence offered the privacy typically associated with a single-family home. There were keyed-access, private elevators leading directly into each residential foyer, and no common walls were shared with a neighbor.

The Aragon offered sprawling single-story condo apartments and two-story townhomes with a private garden, gazebo, pool and spa. In addition, a three-story penthouse crowned each of the three towers and had a rooftop sundeck with pool and spa. All were of lavish proportions, and the views were unforgettable.

Doing things differently, the developers offered a choice of twelve different floor plans with variations of each. This would be a nightmare for most developers, but Brian and Jim seemed unfazed. This meant that no two residences were the same. So, if you are thinking that the bathrooms are "stacked" one above each other in each tower, think again. The plumbing and electrical snaked throughout, from one floor to the next, making it a tremendous construction challenge. But Boca Developers had a staff of architects and engineers to assist buyers in customizing these ready-to-be-finished residences to meet their exacting specifications. Turnkey, furnished models that were ready for immediate occupancy were also available.

Although the partners had purchased the land for the Aragon in 1993 at the height of the savings and loan crisis, buying it on the cheap, they poured whatever they had saved on the land back into construction costs for the project. It was unlikely that they would build another building like it again.

Boca Developers' next project was Townsend Place (which they once tentatively called the Grand Flats at Townsend Place, as a word play on the British "Townsend" name). Three nine-story towers were positioned on a plum parcel of land in downtown Boca Raton, across from the Royal Palm Plaza. The land also fronted the Boca Raton Resort and Club's renovated eighteen-hole golf course.

Brian and Jim were in the forefront of the city's downtown residential transformation. They sought to capture the attention of local residents who owned single-family homes in central or west Boca and now desired a more carefree lifestyle in a recreated city atmosphere. Urban living (and in this case, "Eastward Ho") was just catching on in Boca Raton. If you go to Boca's bustling downtown today, with its plethora of construction projects either completed or under way, you'll see exactly how far this city has come. And those who got in on the ground floor at Townsend Place and purchased there early on, for prices ranging from $220,000 to $700,000, are apt to have experienced tremendous appreciation of their properties.

The Adler Network helped Boca Developers expand their market reach to attract vacation-home buyers from the Northeast too.

Judy had an acquaintance, Teddy Smith from Sharon, Massachusetts, who had relocated to Boca Raton. At the age of fifty, Teddy was one of the first buyers at Townsend Place. Judy interviewed him for an article, which resulted in national coverage in the *Boston Globe*. Unfortunately for him, the coverage was *so* widespread that he told us his ex-wife had discovered where he now lived and asked him for more money! Teddy went on to become the property manager for Boca Developers at Townsend Place and then at Mizner Grand, before he became ill and was met with an untimely death. This was a tremendous loss for the people who knew and admired him.

We also worked with Boca Developers when they brought Mizner Grand to market in the late nineties. The two towers, which tier from twelve to ten floors each, are located on the west side of Lake Boca Raton and offer eight hundred feet of prime lake frontage.

Collectively, the Aragon, Townsend Place, and Mizner Grand projects reportedly had a build-out value exceeding $330 million. During our tenure with the developers, we generated a lot of favorable publicity and held events for prospective buyers and the real estate brokerage community, leading to total sellouts of these elegant properties.

It's About Time

It wasn't an entirely unique idea that Judy had come up with, but Boca Developers liked it and asked us to make it happen. That's why a time capsule has been buried on the site of Townsend Place since January 1997. It was hidden beneath the earth at the same time that groundbreaking for the condominium project took place.

To our knowledge, a time capsule had never been buried in Boca Raton before. Consequently, there was a lot of ballyhoo about it once we got the word out.

We asked a selected list of area organizations and businesses to donate items that would indicate to future treasure hunters what Boca Raton was like in the late nineties. This satisfied the developers' desire to involve the local community of which they were very much a part.

Early on, Judy and I set out on a treasure hunt of our own as we approached these neighboring merchants and organizations. Our efforts yielded floor plan designs from Townsend Place, a Boca Raton Historical Society newsletter, a current issue of the *Boca Raton News*, the 1996–97 business plan from the Boca Raton Chamber of Commerce, cigars from both Bennington Tobacconist and Hampton Tobacco, a luggage tag and other small items from the Boca Raton Resort and Club, a Jacobson's shopping bag from its recent grand opening in Mizner Park, cinema tickets to the AMC Mizner Park Eight Theaters, a menu from Max's Grille, a program from the Royal Palm Dinner Theater, and menus from the Boulevard Grille, French Café, and Espana restaurants in Royal Palm Plaza. Other participants included Publix (when it was under construction just south of East Camino Real at Federal Highway) and Liberties Fine Books.

Much has changed since 1997 in the downtown Boca Raton area. And who knows if anyone plans to unearth this time capsule. Boca Developers anticipated that this would occur twenty-five years from the date it was buried, on January 16, 2022. I hope it will and that I'll be around to witness it!

RESCUE TRAINING

In 1997, we created an opportunity to help Boca Raton and its surrounding communities after construction had recently begun at Townsend Place. One day in March, when the corner of SE Mizner Boulevard and Federal Highway typically would be busy with construction workers laying the foundation for the three new towers, things were different. The construction pit, as it is called, was filled with men who usually see a building *after* it is completed, not *before* it has been built.

We had arranged for the South Florida Urban Search and Rescue Task Force Two to hold a weekly practice session on the site of the future condominium development. The initial phase of construction in the twenty-foot-deep pit was an ideal place for some South Florida fire-rescue departments to practice rigging cables, rappelling, and working with cranes.

The *Sun-Sentinel* was on hand to report on it. Lieutenant John Johnson of Boca Raton Fire-Rescue Services told the reporter, "You can sit in a training room and talk all day, but you don't get experience like this."

The group was there to learn how a building is put together and about the equipment used in the process. So this was a very useful training exercise because it was as realistic as possible. It provided hands-on experience for those rescuers in a controlled setting.

On that day, two members of Task Force Two swung through the air in the iron basket of a 360-foot-high crane, which was being operated by Miller and Solomon, the general contractor for Townsend Place. The two men descended downward into the pit to save a man acting as if he had been caught beneath a concrete slab. The whole scenario was make-believe but effective.

At the time, the Federal Emergency Management Administration (FEMA) had twenty-five task forces nationwide that they activated whenever natural or man-made disasters occurred in urban locations in or outside of the United States. The Task Force Two was especially large, with 172 members from eighteen different South Florida agencies. The regional team consisted of the best and brightest to do the dangerous job required.

In 2004 we coordinated a similar rescue training session but with a different organization, when we represented the Related Group's Aquazul condominium tower in Lauderdale-by-the-Sea. Again, this was a great way to help the local community *and* attract attention to our client's property.

Working with Brian and Jim didn't always go smoothly, particularly for Judy who was working with me on their account. This was the first time since she had joined the Adler Network that we discovered clients sometimes treated her differently than they treated me. I suppose it was because my last name was Adler and hers was not. I felt that this was grossly unfair. She wasn't just some underling. She was vice president of our agency and deserved equal respect. But she didn't always get it. Some examples follow.

While we represented Boca Developers, Jim (who was the more mild mannered of the two partners) told Judy that she *must* get an article about their new properties into the *Sun-Sentinel's* Saturday Real Estate section. Since this was a paid "advertising section," Judy knew it was impossible to get an article placed there—even if we *wrote* it—unless Boca Developers advertised. It was a pay-for-play kind of thing. But they didn't want to advertise in that newspaper at that time. We had maintained a close relationship with the *Sun-Sentinel* for many years and knew this to be a fact. So Judy told Jim the truth.

"We can't do it, Jim, unless you buy an ad."

"Don't you tell me you *can't* do it!" he yelled, standing up and hammering his fist on the table. "Don't you *ever* tell me you can't do it!" This verbal attack was completely out of character for Jim.

My point is that Jim would never have spoken to *me* in that way.

Boca Developers eventually did advertise in that newspaper, and we got them great "advertorial" coverage in addition to editorial coverage in the business section. Jim and Judy also got past that incident.

On another occasion, Brian eviscerated Judy's writing style, even though everything she had produced was correctly written, had been client approved, and being published just about everywhere we submitted it. (There are subtle ways to be critical without beating up on another person.) This fiasco occurred when we were with Brian and Jim in a strategic marketing meeting. The principals of ISG and Beber Silverstein Advertising were also present. Unaccustomed as Judy was to such a reprimand, she sat there like the rest of us, in silence. Her professionalism prevailed.

Brian's insults didn't deflate me. I had seen him go after other people on the marketing team in similar ways in the past, so I knew I wasn't the only one who was the target of his tirades. I also knew that when people dish out criticism in that manner, they embarrass themselves more than they do the objects of their reproach. So I hung in and hung tough.

Brian could be the most charming of charmers when we had him "out front" at one of our events, but I felt he could be a bully in a conference room. Furthermore, when it came to his relationship with the real estate broker community (which is the life blood of *any* developer), I thought that he showed only contempt. This didn't make sense at all. And it didn't sit well with me.

My "Dear John" letter to Brian Street was the third resignation letter I had ever sent during my career of forty-plus years.

Hard Times

Before going out of business, Boca Developers grew to become one of the largest privately held condominium developers in Florida. Brian and Jim remained on the fast track until the late 2000s, when South Florida became an epicenter for the residential market meltdown. The severe downturn cascaded Boca Developers into financial straits. They reportedly owed lenders hundreds of millions of dollars and faced foreclosures woes. My guess is that they had too many projects in the works, and they got in over their heads.

They weren't the only ones. Many projects by other developers never got off the ground. Fortunately, those other developers were able to ride out the storm.

CHAPTER 19

Confrontation amid the Palms

ONE OF MY MOST MEMORABLE stories occurred during the time my agency represented the Palms. Neil Fairman, president and founder of the Plaza Group, was the developer of the project. It consisted of two Mediterranean-style condominium towers and several multi-story villas situated along Fort Lauderdale's beach front, south of Oakland Park Boulevard. Designer Tommy Hilfiger was among investors in this beautiful property, and he planned to have a vacation residence there.

In the late nineties, Judy and I were at a predevelopment marketing meeting with Neil, creative ad man Murray Gaby, and Louise Sunshine of the Sunshine Group (Florida), the firm that was the sole sales and marketing agent for the Palms. Murray, who had once been a pro boxer under a different name, began presenting concepts for an advertising campaign. Louise became critical. Suddenly, Murray went into a rage. He jumped out of his seat, pointed his face and finger an inch from Louise.

"Don't you f—— with me! Don't you ever f—— with me!" he shouted.

So much for decorum during a business meeting.

Neil, Judy, and I simultaneously slid downward in our chairs, afraid to look at one another. Poor Neil was mortified and at a loss of what to do, as we were. Who would believe what had just taken place? Murray apparently still had the spirit of a fighter. He had verbally attacked a branding guru whose skills in predevelopment planning, marketing, and new construction sales were recognized internationally. Louise had been an early employee of the Trump Organization before she went on to found the Sunshine Group in New York in 1986 and the Sunshine Group (Florida) later on. (Years later she became Chairman Emeritus of the Corcoran Sunshine Group, before again starting another company.) Louise was smart, tough, and at times, intimidating. She oftentimes used language that was less than ladylike. Obviously she did not enjoy being on the receiving end. We didn't blame her.

The meeting came to a screeching halt. Louise walked out, and I joined her in the parking lot, followed by Judy who got into my car and waited for me. Meanwhile, Louise began sobbing in fear for her life. "Murray's going to kill me!" she told me. "He'll kill me!"

OMG.

As shocked as I was to see this seemingly hard-as-nails woman become unhinged, and stunned over the confrontation that we had just witnessed, I assured Louise that she was safe and not in danger. After she finally calmed down, I joined Judy in my car to return to the office. Never in all our years as career women had we been in the center of a scenario such as this. Nonetheless, we could not stop laughing.

As we were pulling onto A1A, my car phone rang. Because we were running late, my wonderful, concerned husband was worried that something terrible had happened to us, such as a car accident or even a kidnapping. Over the speaker, Owen was screaming. When he became overly agitated or upset, this was his *modus operandi.* It was simply his way of expressing his emotions, and I preferred that he get them out rather than have a heart attack. But Judy and I still couldn't keep it together. Sometimes levity helps following uncomfortable situations. This was certainly one of them. Not Owen's ranting, but Murray's. We were hysterical and could hardly catch our breaths. Yet somehow I was able to tell my husband that we were fine.

"And honey, have we got a story to tell you! You won't believe what happened at the meeting!"

My words fell upon deaf ears. Owen's yelling continued another few seconds before I said we would see him at the office in less than ten minutes. I then hung up.

"No, Maxine. The drive will take at least twenty-five minutes. You always do this! You underestimate your ETA, and Owen becomes a nervous wreck, worrying and getting wound up all over again," Judy said.

After her reprimand, which I deserved, we continued to talk about what had transpired at the Palms. And in the coming years, whenever we were in Louise's company or saw her on a news program, that remarkable story kept coming back to us.

Certainly it did, in spring of 2016, when we saw Louise on CNN. She was being interviewed about how Donald Trump treats women based on her own past working experience with him. Her response was favorable for the man who, at the time, was the presumptive GOP presidential nominee.

He later would become the forty-fifth US president.

As for Murray, we don't recall if we ever saw him again.

CHAPTER 20
The Quiet Trump

DONALD TRUMP ISN'T THE ONLY Trump leaving a mark on luxury real estate development. A much more restrained Trump, Jules Trump, was among the first to set the bar on luxury condominium living in South Florida when he began building the 80-acre, master-planned Williams Island in the early to mid eighties. Jules had absolutely no financial, philosophical, or familial ties to "the other Trump." Yet it was the low-profile visionary Jules Trump from South Africa who relocated first to New York in the seventies, where he became involved in a number of businesses, one of which was real estate with his bachelor brother Eddie Trump. They subsequently moved to South Florida and left their signature on the skyline here. Jules's delightful wife, Stephanie, was also involved in the family business.

Although the property they had purchased in Aventura was a peninsula, after they built a series of marinas, it became a private island surrounded by a continuous flow of water from Dumfoundling Bay, Maule Lake, and little Maule Lake. In addition, the luxury residences that the Trumps built there were among the first of their kind in the region. Situated between Miami and Fort Lauderdale, the exclusive Williams Island community was a Shangri-La *and* the cornerstone that other developers would emulate for years to come, as condominium fever began sweeping over the region.

Designed to replicate the Italian Riviera, Williams Island (named for Jules and Eddie's father "Willie") was promoted as the "Florida Riviera." Residences nestled within high-rise towers and others set in a charming midrise Mediterranean Village—along with premier resort facilities—lured buyers from all over the world. As previously mentioned in chapter 8, world-class Williams Island made Sophia Loren its "face," giving the private enclave a star-like panache. Among other celebrities who made Williams Island their *home away from home* over the years were singer and actress Whitney Houston, baseball slugger Sammy Sosa, NFL running back Curtis Martin, NFL coach Jimmy Johnson, and jockey Jorge Chavez, to name a few.

During our years working with Williams Island, there were many events for residents, such as those featuring artists Peter Max and Romero Britto, in addition to an evening with actress and songstress Sally Kellerman who had played "Hot Lips O'Houlihan" in the movie *M*A*S*H*. There were mega-yacht and exotic car shows and Easter egg hunts, snow days, hayrides, and rock-climbing walls for kids.

Much of the lifestyle of Williams Island residents revolved around those events. The Trumps planned and paid for them because these were items in their overall marketing budget, designed to increase residential sales. But after the Trump family turned over the community to the master community association (which *all* developers eventually do), those events only continued if the association budgeted and paid for them.

I had been involved with Williams Island early on while representing Ted Fine, the designer who did many of the model interiors there. But my agency wasn't actually retained by the Trump Group until 2000. Starting in that year, we helped director of sales and marketing Michael Goldstein sell out the Residence du Cap and Villa Marina towers. (We knew Michael from when he had worked with the Sunshine Group selling condominiums at the Palms.) At Williams Island, we generated publicity, attended the community's many events, and produced multipage, oversized newsletters, which also included a separate insert directed to real estate brokers.

We produced similar newsletters for other developers too. As marketing tools, they gave reports on development progress and sales information. They also featured activities, events, staff profiles, and buyer testimonials, among other items.

Undoubtedly, one of our biggest triumphs for the Trump Group was being able to get a very favorable cover story in the "Business Monday" section of the *Miami Herald* about Jules Trump and his company's planned fifty-one-story

Acqualina residential and hotel condominium in Sunny Isles Beach. Getting the story wasn't so remarkable. It actually was the story title beneath Jules's photograph on the front page of that business section that made us look really good in his eyes. You see, Jules was the direct opposite of Donald Trump. Jules shied away from the cameras and preferred that his *projects* be in the spotlight. The same could be said for Eddie Trump. So it had taken a lot of convincing for Jules to finally agree to an interview with writer Barbara DeLollis, in 2001. Though he was ready to break his silence about his plans for Acqualina, he still was reluctant to be featured in the media. Because we knew Barbara to be a fair journalist, we took a chance and put the two of them together. But what we *didn't* know, until the morning that issue of the *Miami Herald* was on newsstands, was that she would refer to Jules as "The Quiet Trump." Jules loved it! We had lucked out big time.

Sometimes I would get a conference call on a Sunday afternoon from Jules Trump, and Alan Matus, president of Williams Island Associates Ltd. They would discuss a subject of importance with me, and I then would have to draft a news release, speech, or letter from them to Williams Island residents, which they needed in hand either that evening or by early the next morning. I didn't mind doing this on a weekend because they were respectful—and because they didn't do this too often!

I felt that Jules put a lot of faith in me. He also asked me to proofread everything that his advertising agency was producing, whether it was a brochure, direct mail piece or print advertisement.

In general, I think that Jules put a lot of faith in *people*. He was always anxious to get opinions from those around him, including the Williams Island limousine driver. I respected him for respecting what *everyone* had to say.

The Trumps epitomized *family* to me, and I was impressed when Jules would oftentimes call Eddie during meetings to determine how he felt about the topics we were discussing.

Judy and I got to know Jules and Stephanie on a personal level too. That was even better than knowing them professionally. Although I was not privy to what they had in their bank accounts, I do know they had other holdings elsewhere, such as in New York, California, and Israel that would indicate their success and influence. But you would never know it. The Trumps are warm, caring, and grounded individuals. They love their children and grandchildren just like the rest of us do. They observe Judaism and go to temple. And they are generous donors to many charities. You will read about one of those charities toward the end of this chapter.

One evening, Owen and I were invited over to the Trumps' Williams Island penthouse for dinner. Dr. Barth Green and his wife were there as well. As we dined on the terrace, we had a delightful conversation. First, there was a discussion about Willie Trump's health, which everyone was concerned about. Barth was Willie's physician, as well as serving as the chairman of the Miami Project to Cure Paralysis. We also talked about Ted Fine, who had designed the interiors of the Greens' residence in Miami. I had arranged to have it photographed and featured in a magazine. Meanwhile, as host and hostess, the Trumps couldn't have been more affable or accommodating. And Jules had a terrific sense of humor, so he got along famously with Owen, who was always telling jokes.

When my mother passed away at age ninety two, I was truly moved when Stephanie came to her funeral. She didn't know my mom, but she was there for *me*. I will always remember that act of kindness.

In 2003 when Willie Trump died, Judy, Owen, and I attended his funeral. There was a huge turnout because "Willie" was admired and loved. He was a family man who was down to earth and a pleasure to be around. He also was a jokester. Following his burial at the cemetery, we received very warm hugs from Jules, Eddie, and Stephanie. Those signs of affection were deeply heartfelt and not at all superficial.

Sadly, after Willie's wife Celia passed away a year later, we attended that funeral as well.

One time, Jules asked me if I was married. When I told him that I was divorced, he seemed genuinely concerned—much more concerned than I was! He said he hoped I'd find a special man because I deserved it. (Eventually I did.)

Working with the Trump Group spring boarded the Adler Network deeper into the world of luxury real estate development within Williams Island. We were later retained by Vintage Properties to help market Villa

Flora, by developer Gary Cohen to help market Island Estates, and by WCI Communities to help market the thirty-story BellaMaré tower. In addition, Joel Matus, broker and vice president of Williams Island Realty, hired us to help promote his real estate firm on and off the island.

We also worked with the Trump Group when they introduced Acqualina, and then Luxuria Residences on the ocean in Boca Raton. Acqualina helped transform Sunny Isles Beach from a strip of run-down motels into some of the priciest real estate in South Florida. Luxuria had a very interesting storyline as well. There had been an old condominium building in disrepair on that oceanfront site in Boca. The condominium owners couldn't afford to make the required improvements, so the Trump Group negotiated the purchase of all of the condos in that building from the owners. Subsequently, the building was demolished, and Luxuria replaced it.

We also worked with Jules in the town of Palm Beach, when the Trumps partnered with Gordon Deckelbaum of Premier Developers (under the company name Premier Palm Beach LP) to build Bellaria.

Additional projects that the Trumps are engaged in locally (as of this writing) are the Mansions at Acqualina and the Estates at Acqualina, both in Sunny Isles Beach.

For "The Quiet Trump" and his family, the sky's the limit.

DREAMERS

In 2001, while working with the Trump Group, Stephanie Trump asked us to become involved with the "I Have a Dream" Foundation (IHAD), a program that promises young, at-risk children a state college or vocational school education, if they stay in school and graduate.

We were immediately hooked and began doing pro bono work for the Miami chapter, which Stephanie had founded in 1995. She and her family became sponsors of an entire second-grade class of ninety-seven students at Charles R. Drew Elementary in Liberty City. In keeping with the mission of the national IHAD Foundation, a 501(3) nonprofit organization established in 1981, the Trumps were among those helping children from low-income areas reach their educational and career goals. They provided a comprehensive program of mentoring, tutoring, and life skills enrichment, with an assured opportunity for higher education.

Because I knew African American golf legend Lee Elder from our dealings with Palm-Aire Country Club, I thought he would be an excellent role model for these children. He had been the first black golfer to play at the Masters Tournament and was a Senior PGA Professional. Some said that Lee Elder was to golf what Jackie Robinson was to baseball. They both broke the color barrier in sports that had been traditionally white. When Tiger Woods won his first Masters Tournament in 1997 and was being interviewed, he mentioned Lee Elder.

Lee lived locally, so I called him and asked him to become involved. It didn't take much persuading. He subsequently visited the Dreamers, who in 2001 were eight graders. His objective was to build their self-esteem and inspire them by showing that achieving one's dreams is possible, no matter what the odds. He also encouraged these youth to complete their education so they could go on to lead productive lives. His theme was appropriately "stay the course."

In 2003 Lee also participated in the Pavarini "I Have a Dream" Foundation Golf Tournament in order to help those low-income students realize their dreams of a higher education. It netted the organization $130,000, and took place simultaneously with a tennis classic. Both events followed a gala held on the previous evening. Lee was on hand for the tournament brunch and shotgun tee off, and he eagerly posed for photographs with the charity's many supporters. Many of the Dreamers, who now were tenth graders attending more than ten different area high schools, were there helping Stephanie. She had gotten important sponsors and tirelessly planned and executed all of the components for these events. She was truly amazing. *Too bad she wasn't for hire!*

Best of all, of those ninety-seven Dreamers sponsored by the Trumps, none had been arrested, dropped out of school, or become pregnant. Their academics had improved, and the majority of students had already passed the FCATs.

Then we introduced IHAD to Venus Williams. Knowing that the organization was looking for an exciting national role model and spokesperson, I suggested Venus even though I hadn't met her.

Maxine was always doing this—throwing out a name and not knowing if she could deliver. But of course, she did *deliver. She knew that Venus had founded an interior design firm in Jupiter, Florida, in 2002. So she contacted her.*

Venus was extremely cordial as well as enthusiastic about helping the Dreamers. In 2004, the world-ranked tennis player visited local juniors gathered at Miami Northwestern Senior High School, where she spoke to them.

I was standing next to Venus and recall her asking me, "Judy, what should I say?"

"Speak from your heart, Venus." That's exactly what she did.

This was a dream come true for those students who now were eleventh graders. They were all ears. Approximately thirty of those kids attended Miami Northwestern in Liberty City, while the other sixty seven were enrolled in thirteen other South Florida high schools. Some Dreamer parents also joined the students on that day.

Even off the court, Venus scored points in front of her young audience. She gave an overview of her family life, her schooling, and her career. She then conveyed several poignant messages: Believe in yourself and work hard. Surround yourself with supportive, caring people. Avoid people who distract you and are a negative influence. If you care about yourself, you'll make the right decisions. Give one hundred percent every time so you won't have any regrets. If you lose, work harder. Do whatever it takes to win and achieve your dreams.

For Venus, that meant being a tennis superstar, owning an interior design firm, and becoming a fashion designer.

Meanwhile, Venus's father Richard had accompanied his daughter that day and photographed her every move. It was obvious that he was very proud of her.

Venus also attended a reception to kick off the IHAD Foundation of Miami's annual gala, golf, and tennis tournament scheduled that coming May at the Biltmore Hotel in Coral Gables. The host venue for this reception was the Zodiac Restaurant at Neiman Marcus Bal Harbour. In addition to the delectable hors d'oeuvres and desserts, there was a guitarist, as well a model showing off elegant Badgely Mischka evening gowns. The retailer's new vice president and general manager Lisa Perri-Molina was the perfect hostess.

As you might have guessed, Venus also attended the dinner dance and silent and live auctions at the Biltmore. *There was no question that she was a team player.*

During the time we were involved with IHAD, the Miami chapter had five programs. In addition to the Trumps, sponsors were Norman and Irma Braman, the Sharlin family, and David and Beth Ertel, as well as Bayview Financial (David Ertel and Nancy Hector). In 2004, another class of inner-city students was brought under the wing of the Miami chapter. Fifty-one first graders attending the Phillis Wheatley Elementary School in the Overtown area of Miami began receiving support and were officially adopted as Dreamers. The Trump family and the MBM Family Foundation, represented by Mark and Margie Buchbinder, sponsored the new class. Collectively, the chapter served over five hundred children. It had been Stephanie's efforts that inspired these other philanthropists to join her efforts.

In 2007 the Trump family began sponsoring their third group of Dreamers; those students are slated to graduate high school in 2020. The class is at Hibiscus Elementary School in Miami Gardens.

I think that the Trumps left South Africa because they preferred to live in a country without *apartheid*—and that Stephanie founded the IHAD Miami chapter because she and her family had experienced that terrible separateness while living in South Africa. To this, I say bravo.

CHAPTER 21

Imploded

THE MOST INTERESTING EVENT WE were involved in was bringing down the house—the Harbour House North, that is. The year was 2004.

Built in 1962, the fifteen-story rental tower sat at the northernmost end of Bal Harbour at the Bakers Haulover Inlet—a location that was truly extraordinary. Harbour House North was slated for implosion by WCI Communities in 2004. This was after WCI had entered into a contract to purchase the property on which the new, world-class One Bal Harbour residential and hotel condominium would be constructed. At that time, WCI was Florida's leading builder and developer of highly "amenitized" communities and tower residences.

One Bal Harbour would be the first, true mixed-use project ever to be built in the prestigious village. Situated on Collins Avenue overlooking the ocean and inlet, the new project also would be one of the first new luxury residential condominiums in the village in a decade and the first new hotel to be built there in nearly fifty years.

We were involved in much of the preparation for the implosion, which included attending meetings and interfacing with village officials, officials from nearby municipalities, local police and fire departments, the US Coast Guard, and the Federal Aviation Association. Aircraft would be restricted to flying a minimum of one thousand feet above buildings in the area and five hundred feet offshore. Nearby roads, bridges, and the inlet needed to be temporarily shut down. This was a monumental undertaking, and proper coordination was the key to everyone's safety.

Two days before the implosion took place, the Adler Network held a press briefing and "dynamite" photo opportunity for the media on the actual site where the implosion would take place on that Sunday. We introduced members of the press to WCI executives and the team of demolition and implosion experts. The Loizeaux family, owners of Controlled Demolition Inc. of Phoenix, Maryland, explained the process that would be used to implode Harbour House North, gave out information about temporary road, bridge, and inlet closings, and answered questions.

Other companies involved in the implosion effort were Boran Craig Barber Engel (BCBE) Construction Co. Inc. of Naples, Florida; DPC General Contractors Inc. of Miami; and Omega Contracting Inc. of Pompano Beach.

There's an old saying, "If you build it, they will come." Well, they also came for the implosion, which we hyped heavily through the media, both before and afterward.

WCI hosted a VIP gourmet breakfast before sunrise on the morning of the implosion. It was held at the southeast corner of Haulover Park, which was just north of the inlet and directly across the water from Harbour House North. Invited guests included Florida legislators, village officials, and other high-profile VIPs, as well as the press, all of whom were able to observe history in the making when the implosion followed at eight o'clock in the morning.

We had set up a special media viewing area, then gave out press passes and media kits, and issued a warning that dust generated by the implosion (depending on wind direction and speed) could reach the area in which they were standing. We advised camera personnel to be prepared to cover or put their cameras completely inside some type of case to prevent dust infiltration into their camera and sound equipment. Controlled Demolition explained the timing of the implosion in advance so they knew when to start shooting. There was also a countdown. I communicated via cell phone with television station helicopter pilots in the area, alerting them exactly when the blast was about to take place. Furthermore, after it did, we made digital photography and B-roll footage available, upon request, for media unable to cover the event in person.

Our efforts resulted in news coverage on all of the Miami, Broward, and Palm Beach County television stations, in addition to multiple newscasts on national networks including NBC and FOX News. A total of twenty-six segments were aired, not to mention all of the local pre- and post-implosion print media coverage. Keep in mind this was *before* you could put news information online and the advent of social media.

CSI: Miami filmed the implosion and intended to write the implosion scene into a script for a future episode. Producers of the hit CBS television series had heard about the implosion in advance and flew to Miami to meet with local scouting directors, transportation directors, and WCI representatives to discuss the matter. They then sent a television crew to capture the action with their cameras on the day of the implosion.

The implosion went off perfectly, just as planned. Reminiscent of the Fourth of July, loud blasts thundered through the air as Harbour House North's empty shell disappeared in a colossal cloud of dust. In about sixteen seconds, the old landmark collapsed just left of center, and then the left and right sides folded in on one another. Approximately 660 pounds of carefully placed explosives had brought it down to ground level. Safely.

We had expected to smell something burning. We did not. The odor was of a different nature, something we couldn't describe. What we had not anticipated, however, was that the huge cloud of dust would float from the site northward toward Haulover Park. Each of us on the Adler Network team was wearing black pants, a black jacket, black shoes, and a surgical mask, which became completely covered with gray powder. Nonetheless, we were exhilarated!

The demise of the Harbour House North stirred up memories for people who had once rented an apartment there. It also created a "neat" mess (if that is possible). It was very much controlled and restricted to the site. Giant piles of crumbled concrete and mangled metal took clean-up subcontractors about three months to remove, before WCI started construction on One Bal Harbour, which we subsequently referred to as the New Northern Gateway to Bal Harbour.

CHAPTER 22

There's Never Been a Better Time to Buy

REAL ESTATE HAS ALWAYS BEEN a cyclical industry, subject to market peaks and downturns. Since most of the Adler Network's business depended upon real estate development and sales, which in turn affected architects, interior designers, and home furnishing companies, our firm had been in jeopardy several times over the decades. Fortunately, we were able to survive each slump. And we benefited from every uptick.

Real estate makes up a large segment of the total wealth of the South Florida economy. Booms are oftentimes accompanied by periods of extreme speculation involving the expansion of credit. When the bubble bursts, an entire region suffers. This was the case in South Florida and elsewhere throughout the United States, after the most recent housing bubble wreaked havoc. Home and condominium prices had reached their heights in early 2006 and then started to deteriorate that same year as well as the next. By the end of 2008, the Case-Stiller home price index reported that housing prices had suffered the largest drop in its history. And lower prices continued.

This wasn't just a hiccup. The housing bubble burst, storming through like a hurricane. The resulting financial crisis led to the Great Recession, which spanned from December 2007 to June 2009. For one thing, there was the greed of Wall Street for packaging and selling residential mortgaged-backed securities. For another, lenders had eased underwriting requirements, and their lackadaisical policies allowed buyers with impaired credit to receive low introductory-rate mortgages that would go much higher. Furthermore, government regulators failed to crack down on those predatory lending practices. The subprime-mortgage-market meltdown and a landslide of foreclosures came next, followed by a collapse in consumer spending and business investment, the loss of jobs, and disintegrating family incomes. All of this posed a grave risk to the US economy.

In 2007 it became evident that the housing and credit markets were plummeting. We were on the way to a catastrophe. But rather than sit back on our haunches and wait for the tide to turn, the Adler Network became proactive. We simply couldn't rest idly and watch the free fall. We tried to minimize it. More about that in a minute.

As if things weren't bad enough, one of the country's top national home builders stated in an article something such as, "Why should I pay for hay when there are no horses to eat it?" He was referring to paying for advertising and public relations services when the housing market was plunging downward and out of control. Likewise, I thought that a *Palm Beach Post* reporter also made the situation worse with his flow of negative doom-and-gloom articles. I know it is best for the editorial and advertising departments of a newspaper to be separate, but perhaps there should be some exceptions. Also, I felt that those pessimistic articles must have negatively impacted the *Post's* advertising revenues. Fewer builders were buying ads.

There had to be some light at the end of the tunnel, even if it was a small ray of sunshine. Judy and I were determined to find it. We soon came up with a plan to hold two back-to-back real estate forums in October 2007. Since the home furnishings company Robb & Stucky was a client of ours, we were able to hold these forums free of charge in their community rooms. The first forum was in Palm Beach Gardens and the second in Boca Raton. We personally invited area real estate developers, condo and home builders, Realtors, and newspaper advertising representatives. We purposely did *not* invite editorial staff reporters because we needed to get up close and personal about the situation facing South Florida. It was purely for the comfort of our attendees that we did this. We had a total of about sixty people at both forums, including builders, developers, builder and Realtor association representatives, as well as several real estate attorneys, mortgage brokers, and architects. Everyone agreed this was an excellent response.

The overall theme of our forums, or "think tanks" as I preferred to call them, was "There's never been a better time to buy [a home or condominium]." It was echoed by all of our scheduled speakers. They communicated this message and encouraged others to pass it along. Prices can't get much lower. The market had bottomed out. Since no one has been buying, when people do resume their purchases, there will be a pent-up demand, which will improve the market. *Of course, at the time, no one knew that it had* not *bottomed out.*

I welcomed each audience and discussed all the negative press about the housing market and how perception had become reality. Although the news wasn't *all* bad, the bad included whatever reporters were writing about. "There needs to be a more level playing field," I said. Plus, I knew that some good can come out of a problem. It is called *opportunity*.

Two of our guest speakers were retired. They could have declined our invitation to speak and easily played a round of golf instead. Ron Kukulski, former *Sun-Sentinel* real estate advertising manager and publisher of the *Florida New Homes & Condo Guide*, was one of them. The other was John Thomson, a former vice president of the Kolter Property Group. They still retained their passion for the real estate industry, and we felt indebted to them for their participation.

Ron noted how everyone was being affected by the real estate market slowdown because the housing industry was the fuel that drove the engine. Builders must approach and empower their builder associations to go to area newspapers and ask for very low rates for full-page ads, he said. Ads should consistently convey the overall message. Realtors need to empower their associations to approach newspapers and request the same low rates and then run association ads or advertorials consistent with the same message. Lastly, developers and builders should chip in a few thousand dollars each in order to cover advertising design, production, and placement costs.

The result was a "Buy Now" ad campaign in the *Sun-Sentinel*, *Palm Beach Post*, and the *Scripps Treasure Coast Newspapers*. Only the *Miami*

Herald didn't send representatives to either forum or participate with us. They didn't tell us why.

John Thomson suggested a Super Boomer promotion for January 2008 in which new home builders would reduce prices by at least twenty percent from 2005 pricing. Real estate brokers would convince sellers to reduce listing prices by ten percent, and they would reduce their own commissions by one percent. Participating mortgage brokers would offer thirty-year fixed rate mortgages at 5.99 percent and no closing costs to *qualified* buyers. All participants would be listed in full-page newspaper ads beginning on January 1, as well as on websites and in collateral materials for the promotion. There would be a fee to cover expenses. The cut-off date would be at the end of 2009, providing an incentive for buyers and sellers to act quickly.

Other forum speakers included Joey Eichner, president of Catalfumo Development and Management (Catalfumo was a client of ours) and Eric Wallberg, managing partner with WCS Lending in Boca Raton. They each presented informative data and revved up the audience.

Furthermore, we provided the text for a letter we wanted attendees and large groups to send to Florida legislators to convince them that Florida was in need of property tax relief. We also gave them the mailing address and e-mail address of each representative. As I recall, one of the Realtor associations embarked on a letter-writing campaign.

The Adler Network had always enjoyed a special relationship with the people who produced the "Real Estate Weekend" section at the *Palm Beach Post*. In fact, on numerous occasions they came to our office for lunch and a brainstorming session. It was a win-win for all parties concerned. Because their writing staff had been severely cut back due to early retirements and lay-offs, they were responsive to our "pitch" to provide them with interesting and informative real estate and design-related articles. We also had great photos and other graphics from clients to accompany those articles. These ran the gamut from ghost-written guest columns to articles about model homes, new floor plans on the market, specific design features, and the like. At one time (when real estate was booming and the section was very large), Judy wrote the majority of the content. We continue to be grateful to Michelle Bernzweig,

Katie Diets, Tanya Wade, Perry Grant, Chris DeStefano, and others for their receptiveness. We truly loved each of them.

When faced with the mortgage debacle, the *Post* graciously published a guest column that Judy had penned for Eric Wallberg from WCS Lending. He wasn't our client, but we showcased him as an expert anyhow. *If we could fill editorial space and help out our media colleagues, we always seized the opportunity to do so.* On this occasion, the result was an article in December 2007 about the lack of common sense in recent lending practices. However, the content conveyed that *if* people were indeed qualified, they *could* obtain conventional mortgage financing. The funds were available.

During this time, Garrett Foster was responsible for all of the content in the "New Homes" section of the *Sun-Sentinel*. He also was a close colleague of ours. Like us, Garrett was concerned about what was happening to the real estate sector. Consequently, he allowed Judy to write (under the name Lauren Silver, one of her pseudonyms) a three-part series of hard-hitting articles dispelling common myths about the present-day housing market. The objective was to explain and give reasons why those who were qualified *should* buy a home now, even in the current economic climate. Those articles ran weekly in May 2008. Then in June of that same year, Garrett also published Judy's article about builders' furnished models, which are a powerful selling tool. In July, another article followed outlining why home buying at that time made a lot of sense. All of these articles were meant to turn negatives into positives.

The *Sun-Sentinel, Scripps Treasure Coast Newspapers*, and the now-defunct *Boca Raton News* published their own positive stories as well.

This was a huge team effort, and although we couldn't measure if our actions made a difference, at least we knew we had stood up, rallied the troops, and *tried* to make a difference.

In doing so, we also strengthened our agency's brand.

CHAPTER 23

Taking Its Toll

OUR AGENCY BEGAN REPRESENTING TOLL Brothers' new Southeast Florida residential communities in 2000. We felt privileged to have earned the confidence of the nation's leading builder of luxury homes, and over the next seven years, we helped market a total of ten Toll Brothers' properties: The Preserve and Trieste in Boca Raton; Mizner Country Club in Delray Beach; The Estates at Heron Bay in Coral Springs; Toll Brothers at Ibis in West Palm Beach; Beach Front and Ocean's Edge on Singer Island; Frenchman's Reserve in Palm Beach Gardens; Jupiter Country Club in Jupiter; and Palm Cove Golf & Yacht Club in Palm City.

We first worked locally with Dan Grosswald and Kathleen Murphy, two great professionals who we later heard married one another. We had no inkling that they had been romantically involved.

Down the road, other executives in charge of the Southeast Florida region, as well as their project managers, became our go-to persons. We also developed relationships with the Toll Brothers' corporate managers who handled national marketing and public relations from the company headquarters in Pennsylvania.

In addition to touting the features and benefits of Toll Brothers' residences and their accompanying lifestyles, we provided extensive publicity for the grand opening of four signature golf courses: the Arnold Palmer–designed courses at both Mizner Country Club and Frenchman's Reserve, the Chi Rodriguez–designed course at Palm Cove, and the Greg Norman–designed course at Jupiter Country Club. Press conferences and special events commemorated these occasions, and the media turnout was fabulous due to the sports celebrity component.

We also held Media Days at these new courses so that local sports editors, writers, producers, and broadcasters could play on them without charge. Judy and I enjoyed hanging out with these guys, even though we weren't golfers ourselves.

The Greg Norman press conference, in particular, stands out in my mind because it occurred soon after he and his new wife Chris Evert had parted ways. Reportedly, they each had left their previous spouses and enjoyed a glamorous courtship before they married in 2008. The breakup took place between the Australian world golf champion (*aka* "The Great White Shark") and the tennis legend approximately fifteen months after they had tied the nuptial knot.

We had been given a directive in advance and gave the press an important heads up: You may ask Mr. Norman any questions about Jupiter Country Club and the course that he designed, but *under no circumstances* should you ask him questions about his personal life.

What's that saying? There's always one bad apple in the bunch. So the press conference was cut short when a member of the media (from ESPN, I think) questioned him about his marriage. Greg simply thanked everyone and left the podium. He was very much of a gentleman, and we felt badly that this had occurred.

As a publicly traded company, Toll Brothers asked us to provide monthly and annual reports showing the PR value of what we had accomplished for them. Judy had to measure the column inches of all publicity (editorial coverage) that we generated, as well as advertorials (paid articles)—a very labor-intensive task—and then affix a value equivalency to what the cost in advertising dollars would have been if the company had to *purchase* that amount of space. As an example, in our full fiscal year report for 2006, the total advertising equivalency for editorial coverage for the year was $864,159. The valuation was based on current ad rate cards. This comparable advertising expenditure was nearly twenty times the Adler Network's retainer fee for securing articles over the twelve-month period. Then when we applied the Public Relations Society of America's most conservative standard (three times), actual PR value for this editorial coverage in southeast Florida was almost $2.6 million. Furthermore, while this encompassed print and online coverage, it did not include the value of television coverage or advertorial placements.

In spite of working for what (in our opinion) was a low monthly retainer fee for each of Toll Brothers' projects over the years, when the Great Recession loomed, the company asked us to reduce our current fees. We wanted to maintain our working relationship with a national builder because it enhanced our credentials. So we negotiated a reduction in fees that we could live with on a temporary basis. Then there was another reduction. Shortly after, we received another reduction request.

Although the Adler Network had always managed to weather the cyclical slumps in the real estate market over the years, we couldn't possibly continue to put forth our time and efforts without some type of compensation that we considered to be fair. We had office rent and salaries to pay along with other expenses. So we amicably parted ways.

The journey with Toll Brothers had been a very enjoyable one, until providing our services at what we believed to be below-market rates had finally taken its toll on us.

CHAPTER 24

Events R Us

ALONG WITH CREATING OR BOOSTING brand recognition, generating favorable publicity, and making the "right" connections for our clients, the Adler Network could have been called "Events R Us."

Guests commented favorably about our events. And when invited, the media enjoyed attending and covering them because we did a great job of planning, coordinating, and executing them. Each event was a big responsibility, whether it showcased a new model residence for a developer, marked the grand opening of a condominium project or an entire community, or educated brokers and agents during a small broker breakfast. We also held events at the home furnishings showrooms we represented over the years.

When Judy joined the agency, our events got even better. She devised a multiple-page Party Checklist with *every* conceivable component for a successful event, no matter how large or small. She also came up with an abbreviated, one-page sheet that included each component for each event, along with vendor contact information. This served as a reminder of what actions everyone involved needed to take on the day or evening of an event. Judy even sent out e-mails to client representatives and vendors a few days before every event, reminding them of their individual responsibilities. Then upon arrival at an event, she passed out timelines. These were terrific organizational tools that made our events nearly flawless. If there was a glitch or two during an event, only *we* knew about it.

Maxine was like Perle Mesta, the Washington, DC, socialite known for hosting political events—except that the only political event Maxine had ever hosted was for now-retired Broward County Court Judge Marty Dishowitz. He was Maxine and Owen's neighbor in Plantation when he first ran for the Plantation City Council in 1985. Owen ran his campaign and Marty won.

At every one of our clients' events, Maxine was upfront and personal. She greeted and shook everyone's hand, which is an enigma to me because she is some-what of a germophobe.

"Hello. I'm Maxine Adler. Welcome to (project name)." That was her man-tra. I too would sometimes greet guests but preferred being in the main event area so I could keep an eye on the vendors to make certain there were no problems. During each event, I would also work with Maxine to ensure that our clients were photographed with the "appropriate" guests. If there were speeches, I would take notes. These would be used for our follow-up publicity efforts.

Nothing felt better than bringing all of the event components together and having them be absolutely perfect. I oftentimes borrowed Jackie Gleason's phrase "How sweet it is!" to describe the feeling.

When real estate was on an upswing, it wasn't unusual for the Adler Network to be coordinating as many as four events per week. It was an ex-hausting marathon, but satisfying nonetheless.

Most of those events were held in the evenings, so we would work straight through from early morning until midnight. Then, we'd wake up and do that all over again. And because Maxine and I were always wearing high heels, we'd sometimes suffer from debilitating charley horses in our legs after the events ended. This was particularly true after we had walked around an eight thousand seven hundred seventy-square-foot penthouse for four or five hours, as we straightened out draperies and fluffed the pillows and then "worked the room."

Aside from the special events I talk about in previous chapters, here are some additional ones that stand out front and center in my memory.

SECOND RENAISSANCE

In October 1997 we held an event for the Palms oceanfront condominium enclave in Fort Lauderdale. It was called the "Second Renaissance" because it marked the start of sales for the second tower. The East Tower (II) would be thirty-one stories in height.

More than four hundred buyers, local officials, and the members of the press joined designer Tommy Hilfiger (an investor in the project), a group of Asian businessmen, and Neil Fairman, president of the Plaza Group, several floors up on the construction site. With the help of the event décor and entertainment company, Rafael and Juliana Productions, we had transformed raw wide-open concrete space (the shell of the new building) into a "Medieval Venetian Extravaganza," as the invitation had promised. Guests were greeted by torchbearers and trumpeters and entertained by juggling jesters and mimes, all of whom comprised the merry makers of the Royal Court. Champagne flowed freely, and there was a bounty of food from the King's Table. This was all in keeping with the Palms' Mediterranean Revival architecture.

Willing guests were given a ride on a three-hundred-foot tower crane in order to see the glorious panoramas from the site, which included four hundred fifty feet of ocean shoreline, as well as the Intracoastal Waterway and the greenery of Birch State Park. Larry Jankins of the Plaza Group orchestrated these rides. There was a lot of interest.

The Second Renaissance event went off without a hitch, unlike the First Renaissance event that had commemorated the start of sales in the thirty-story South Tower (I). On that particular night, there was a tropical storm with torrential rains and fierce winds. Developer Neil Fairman was a nervous wreck, but we assured him the show must and would go on. In spite of the inclement weather conditions, we still had cars backed up along A1A waiting to arrive. Guests remained patient in anticipation of what was to come. As you might predict, we had to make a few last-minute changes. One of them was having valet parking attendants greet guests while carrying giant golf umbrellas. The umbrellas were substitutes for the fiery torches that costumed entertainers were supposed to have held.

NIKE SOUTH FLORIDA CLASSIC

When the Nike Tour was planning its first event in southeast Florida, the 1998 Nike South Florida Classic, the Adler Network worked closely with representatives from the PGA Tour to make sure everything would run smoothly.

We became involved as the public relations voice, generating publicity before, during, and after the event because of our client, Palm-Aire Country Club in Pompano Beach. At the time, Palm-Aire was the largest country club in the region. It already was hosting the annual Florida Open. Now Palm-Aire had been named the host site for the Nike four-day golf tournament scheduled in January. Of Palm-Aire's four championship courses and one executive course, play would take place on its Palms course. Congressmen Robert Wexler and Mark Foley were named honorary cochairmen.

We worked hand in hand with dynamo Gary Collins, the country club's president and general manager, as well as with the Golf Channel (they were providing over twelve hours of national television exposure) and the Adam Walsh Children's Foundation, which was the benefiting charity. We coordinated all of the media, making sure they were invited, had a proper on-site work area, and given "working press" passes and press kits.

Although we were confident we'd garner a lot of good press for this event, we lucked out and got even more than anticipated because of Casey Martin, one of the players. The young golfer suffered from a rare birth defect in his right leg that made walking so painful that he couldn't get around the course on foot. Because of damage to his leg bone, he also lived with the fear of getting a fracture that could lead to his leg being amputated. With Casey's career as a golfer at stake, he was able to get a federal court order allowing him to ride in a golf cart during the tournament. But it had been a tradition for professional golfers to walk a golf course, and many golf legends, such as Arnold Palmer, were opposed to Casey being the exception. Consequently, due to the controversy, Casey Martin became a very big sports story. When he played here in South Florida, it was covered by CNN, ESPN, *Sports Illustrated,* the Associated Press, the *New York Times,* the *Washington Post,* and numerous local media outlets.

Judy and I worked together on this event, which raised thousands of dollars in donations for the Adam Walsh Children's Fund. This enabled the nonprofit organization to continue its efforts to locate missing children and to stop exploiting them. In addition, the event attracted over one hundred fifty Nike Tour golfers, approximately eighty members of the media from around the country, and twenty thousand spectators. This large turnout contributed nearly $11 million to the tricounty economy. (In an earlier economic impact analysis, the City of Pompano Beach had expected an impact of just over $6 million.) We were very proud of the results. But Judy was even prouder after she received a letter from Bob Hyde of the PGA Tour.

"Congratulations on a great job! I have been in the PR business since 1977 and can honestly say that the efforts of you and the Adler Network staff matched the top performance of any agency I have witnessed."

Owen and I gave Judy another raise.

Years later, in 2006, while serving the sixteenth District of Florida, US Rep. Mark Foley resigned in disgrace amid a political scandal. He was accused of having sent sexually suggestive e-mails and instant messages to young men who had formerly been Congressional pages.

Palm-Aire also hosted the 1999 Nike South Florida Classic. This time, the televised tournament was held on Palm-Aire's newly restored Mighty Oaks course.

Gary Collins at Palm-Aire eventually went on to become the general manager at Toll Brothers' Frenchman's Reserve community in Palm Beach Gardens. Our paths crossed again when Toll Brothers became our client.

A CELEBRATION OF ART, ARCHITECTURE, AND LIFE

To mark the sales success of the Trump Group's Acqualina Ocean Residences and Resort, we staged another Italian Renaissance-themed event. It took place on the site of Williams Island's former Ocean Club in Sunny Isles Beach, where the soaring Acqualina condominium hotel would rise along the Atlantic coastline.

Already seventy percent of the residential condominiums had been purchased by some of the most successful people in the world, without a shovel having been put into the ground. Indeed there was a reason to celebrate.

This event was on a far grander scale than we had ever done before due to the budget that the Trump Group had given us. In addition, we were told that Acqualina's architecture would rival that of Rome or Paris, with interiors inspired by the great palaces of Europe. So this celebration had to be over the top.

In keeping with Acqualina's Italian-inspired Old World design, the site was turned into an enchanting setting replete with Venetian-costumed mimes, trumpeters, torchbearers, heralders (who shouted out the names of arriving guests), stilt walkers, classical "living" statues, unique "garden" figures including a "living" fountain, and a gondolier entertaining guests from a gondola in the existing swimming pool. A harpist, Renaissance musicians, opera singers from the Gold Coast Opera, and culinary specialties served beneath a large decorated tent made this event truly a spectacle. There was nothing tasteless or garish about it; it was elegant. Because of all of the interesting visuals and a ribbon cutting by Mayor Dave Samson, the paparazzi had their cameras flashing all evening long. But it was Acqualina purchasers, local dignitaries and other guests—dressed to the nines in black-tie attire—that truly made this evening memorable.

There was one more thing. It was a very windy night, with breezes coming in from the ocean. I can still remember panicking as I saw flames from the torchbearers being blown on top of the tent. It was as if those flames were dancing! I did some serious praying at that moment. It wasn't until the following day that I found out the tent was flame retardant.

You may be asking yourself, "Why did the Adler Network repeat this Italian theme? Couldn't they have been more creative?"

We employed the same theme for many of our events because it was compatible with Italian-inspired architecture and interior design that was popular for many new real estate projects in South Florida during those years. We had expert vendors to help us create a themed environment of this nature. And the guest lists were always different from one project to another. Only the invited real estate brokers might have been the same, but they loved going to parties, no matter what! Invite them, and they will come.

Even though the real estate market was on fire at this time and developers appeared to have had money to burn, we always tried to save them money. So, as it turned out, we entertained top area brokers and their sales associates on the same Acqualina site on the following evening. We repeated the event, only on a much smaller scale. Because all the elements were already in place, this was cost effective for our client.

In 2005 we planned another elaborate Italian-inspired, thematic, and inter-active event, "A Magical Evening in Italy," for the real estate broker community at the new Luxuria oceanfront property in Boca Raton on behalf of the same developer, the Trump Group.

WORLD-CLASS WINE TASTING

In 2003 we helped market WCI Communities' One Bal Harbour residential and hotel condominium overlooking the ocean and Bakers Haulover Inlet. Because the project wasn't built yet, we selected the Sea View Bal Harbour Hotel for a world-class taste of "Your New World—One Bal Harbour" and invited people who were on the reservation list to purchase a residence at One Bal Harbour. These condominiums were pricey; therefore, sophistica-tion, a high level of service, and attention to every detail were very much in order. We also wanted to reinforce excitement, so when it was time for these reservation holders to go to contract, they would sign on the line without hesitation.

We brought in a Guest Ambassador for the evening, Rob Mondavi, of the renowned Mondavi Winery. Displays of "New World Wines" and "New World Cuisine" were feasts for the eyes as well as the palate. The young and handsome Mondavi was also very easy on the eyes.

For some reason that neither Maxine nor I understood, Francesca McFeely, WCI's regional sales and marketing director, didn't seem to like me. While her boss, John Manrique, WCI's marketing vice president, was a pleasure to work with, in our opinion she was not. Francesca also sometimes wore heavy makeup and very short skirts—not at all in keeping with WCI's more conservative image. Since we were getting a lot of positive exposure for One Bal Harbour and putting on great events, we were perplexed about Francesca's criticism of me, especially in front of other people. Once, in a planning meeting for this event, I came within ten seconds of excusing myself and making a ladylike exit, which would have left

Maxine behind to handle Francesca's unwarranted attacks. Instead, I breathed deeply and kept my cool. Fortunately, the meeting broke up shortly after that.

There's a reason we are sharing this. On the night of this wine-tasting event, even though Maxine, I, and our vendors had arrived early in the morning to begin setting up the Sea View ballroom, Francesca strolled in about ten minutes before the event was to start. As soon as she entered the ballroom, she began complaining about how the room had been staged. She then yelled directives to our vendors to make changes. This put those vendors in an awkward and uncomfortable position, since they had followed a client-approved diagram.

After Francesca's diatribe ended and a few minor tweaks to the ballroom had been made, the doors to the event finally opened, half an hour late. Throughout our years in business, we had never held an event that didn't start early or on time.

I assure you that the venue was exquisite and required *no* changes whatsoever. It looked perfect to us. Designs by Sean, an award-winning full-service event décor company, had done a bang-up job. Upon entering, guests were greeted by a classical guitarist and a "living display" (a beautiful girl with a cascading headdress, who was positioned in the center of a round table, with only her body visible from the waist up). She was surrounded by wine glasses for guests to carry with them. Those glasses were then tagged with their names at a reception table.

A false wall of cascading white fabric, on which theatrical lighting cast colorful auroras behind One Bal Harbour logos in white light, had been created inside the ballroom. Just inside the entry, the WCI logo was projected in white onto the carpet. Throughout the room, there were cozy seating areas with plush white sofas, ottomans, occasion chairs with beaded and jeweled covers slipped onto the backs, and white-draped tables.

The seating areas were surrounded by four wine regions (theatrical "sets"), each designed, illuminated, and appointed to recreate the look and mood of its region's culture, native colors, fabrics, and geography. Every region had a long serpentine table swagged in white fabric, offering two wines from the region, as well as displays of the wine's grapes and items representative of its bouquet. There was a bounty of delicacies that were paired with the wines.

Dramatic florals and artifacts were isolated with pin lights. The food presentations at each table could have been stylized feasts from *Gourmet Magazine*.

It gets even better. Behind the false white-curtained walls, there were three hidden Showcase Presentations on raised platforms, spaced around the room's perimeter. Each featured a very special or rare wine.

There were rinsing stations too, with a white-gloved attendant who rinsed each guest's glass with Evian water as needed. He also dabbed the rim of each glass on a white linen napkin, so that guests could reuse their glasses throughout the evening.

Rob Mondavi presented several of his family's finest and rarest wines. He had a charming repartee and his presentation was peppered with humorous anecdotes. At predetermined intervals, he drew attention to one of the Showcases, and there was a dramatic change in lighting and music. The curtains opened to reveal a vignette depicting the region from which that particular wine originated. He described the vintage, its history and characteristics before a procession of servers filed out from behind the set, each carrying a bottle of the wine and circulating the room to pour samples. Another procession of servers appeared carrying silver platters of the wine's paired cuisine.

The entire evening was underscored by a quartet of musicians playing sophisticated, soothing New Age music. And as guests departed and the valets brought their cars around, a parting gift was on the seat: a large basket with a very collectible bottle of champagne and two Tiffany champagne flutes.

Every element of this one-of-a-kind event had been designed to thank reservation holders and symbolize the unique lifestyle they could expect at One Bal Harbour. We had pulled out all the stops so that guests would know that WCI does it right. The event was very well received by guests, who also included Bal Harbour Village officials and select media.

Several years later, Maxine and I ran into Francesca at an event of ours for another developer. She no longer worked for WCI, and we think she may have been selling real estate. She had on less make up, had her now long hair pulled back into a simple ponytail, and there was no sign whatsoever of a miniskirt. We were, of course, cordial to one another.

Chef Michelle Bernstein

That same year we held another event for One Bal Harbor and called it "A Taste of the Future." Guests were invited to "Journey into the future of imaginable indulgences, reserved only for a fortunate few who will call One Bal Harbour 'home.'"

We promised that inventive cuisine would be art, masterfully prepared by Miami's celebrated Chef Michelle Bernstein. At the time, she was a hot up-and-comer. Her sophisticated *haute* cuisine had already been singled out by *Esquire Magazine*, and she had co-hosted the Food Network series *Melting Pot*. She once battled on the *Iron Chef America* versus Bobby Flay and won. (She had other distinctions at the time and would receive a James Beard Foundation Award in 2008. Her success continues, and we are pleased to have known her.)

Held at the One Bal Harbour Sales and Model Center, housed within Harbour House South (the sister rental property of Harbor House North), the evening began with a cocktail reception and moved on to a sit-down dinner with white-glove service. Among delectable offerings were slices of pan-roasted foie gras with a moscato bianco reduction and glazed California figs (first indulgence), Chef Bernstein's Latin bouillabaisse with fish and shellfish served in a Latin-style saffron broth (pescado), roasted beef tenderloin with fresh truffles, porcini, chanterelles and hen-of-the-woods mushrooms, and red wine reduction sauce (entrée), and warm caramelized apple and chocolate tart, dulce de leche ice cream, and candied pineapple sauce (world-class finish). Each course was paired with a different wine.

My mouth is still watering.

All That Jazz

When Robb & Stucky planned to open a home furnishings store in Mizner Park on the site previously occupied by Jacobson's department store, the Adler Network was hired to represent the company in southeast Florida. We also were asked to create a grand opening event for this new Boca Raton location. The year was 2003.

To debut the eighty thousand-square-foot furniture showroom and interior design studio at Mizner Park, we had our work cut out for us. Our goal was to have as many as two thousand guests, but the logistics and parking could be problematic.

I contacted City Hall and the City of Boca Raton Police Department and somehow convinced them to close down one side of one block on Plaza Real. They were very accommodating, unlike some municipalities I had worked with through the years.

Maxine succeeded again. I had lived in the downtown area and knew that Mizner Park was the city's retail and cultural centerpiece. I had only seen road closings during select art festivals or other city-coordinated special events. Maxine was confident and gutsy, and those traits always benefited our clients. Furthermore, rather than people resenting her, I think she was admired for her moxie.

Because the film *Chicago* had won six Oscar awards, including Best Picture at the Seventy-fifth Academy Awards ceremony just months before, our event theme proved to have perfect timing: "All That Jazz." The title of that song from *Chicago* was projected in lights onto the facade of the Robb & Stucky building. With the help of costumed performers from La Mystique entertainment troupe and classic automobiles from Ragtop Motorcars, we re-created the era of the Roaring Twenties, complete with live jazz entertainers, butlered delicacies, fine wines, and martinis. Meanwhile, visitors viewed two levels filled with beautiful furniture and accessories, not to mention learning about the company's interior design capabilities.

And, yes. Two thousand guests *did* attend this glittering evening.

Robb & Stucky went on to open other retail showrooms in Palm Beach Gardens and Coral Gables, as well as Robb & Stucky Patio stores, which also became clients of ours.

Venetian Street Festival

One of the largest events we ever planned (in terms of the number of guests) was the 2007 grand opening of Kolter Communities' three-thousand-acre master-planned Verano in Port St. Lucie. Billed as "Your New Hometown,"

Verano was offering a desirable, amenity-rich residential experience for a lot less money than one would find in Palm Beach, Broward, or Miami-Dade counties. On that day, the community would unveil fourteen decorator single-family detached and attached model residences, all with Italian designs. Our objective was for every visitor to tour the new homes along Model Row.

This Venetian Street Festival was more casual than our evening affairs had been, but nevertheless it was a mammoth undertaking because of the size of the event area, the logistics, and the parking challenges. Yet somehow we pulled it off at the request of Craig Perna, Kolter's president of east coast planned communities. Craig was a great guy, and we enjoyed working with him.

Visitors picked up a "Passport to Verano" at the registration tent. As they went through each model, their passports were stamped. By turning in their passports with all pages validated, they were then entered into a drawing for a twelve-day Crystal "Splendors of the Mediterranean" cruise to Rome, Civitavecchia, Florence, Livorno, Portofino, Monte Carlo, Monaco, Sicily, Taormina, Corfu (Greece), Dubrovnik (Croatia), and Venice. That valuable incentive attracted a lot of interest from guests who visited all of the model homes.

In keeping with the community's picturesque Old-World landscapes (which emulated an Italian countryside), the entertainment and food at this event were Italian-inspired as well. We had hired Silver Sac very often for their catering services, and they did an absolutely amazing job feeding and quenching the thirst of the thousands of people who attended the Verano event on that day.

We had a confirmed guest count of five thousand visitors. We know this to be factual because valet attendants (dressed as Venetian gondoliers) kept track of the arriving guests.

CHAPTER 25

I'm Not Dead Yet

IT WAS A SUNNY SUMMER day in 2009 at the Boca Beach Club. Judy and I were participants in an all-day marketing meeting for One Thousand Ocean. At the time, this modern architectural landmark was under construction overlooking the Boca Raton Inlet.

We were sitting to the left of Jamie Telchin, president of development for LXR Luxury Resorts. Although Jamie generally avoided taking phone calls during meetings, his cell phone rang just as the meeting had begun, and he answered it when the name Wendy Larsen appeared on the screen. Most of us knew Wendy not only for her land-use planning and zoning legal expertise, but also for her involvement in furthering culture and the arts in the downtown Boca Raton area.

"Hello, Wendy. I'm in a meeting. What's up?"

Jamie remained silent as Wendy told him she had just heard very disturbing news. We could see his demeanor change.

"Maxine Adler was struck by a car and killed in a hit-and-run accident while walking across North Federal Highway near Yamato Road," she told him.

Both relieved and somewhat amused, Jamie said, "I don't think so."

"What do you mean, you don't think so? Jamie, I am telling you that Maxine Adler died!"

"And I'm telling you again, Wendy, Maxine did *not* die."

"Well, how can you be so sure?" she asked him.

"Because Maxine is sitting next to me right now." End of conversation. Lots of laughter. The meeting continued.

As it turned out, there was another Maxine Adler, similar in age to me, who also lived in Boca Raton. A *Sun-Sentinel* article revealed that she had a home in the Sanctuary as well as another residence in California. The driver of the SUV that had struck her down had been caught by police, thanks to an eye witness who remembered the license plate information.

When I answered my home phone that evening, a reporter from the news department at one of the Palm Beach County television stations asked to speak to a member of the Adler family.

"This is Maxine Adler," I said. "How can I help you?"

"No, no, no. You don't understand," the voice said. "I'd like to speak to someone in the immediate family *about* Maxine Adler."

"I *do* understand, and I am telling you that *I* am Maxine Adler."

"But, according to a police report, Maxine Adler was the victim of a fatal hit-and-run auto accident," the voice insisted.

"And I am telling you, for the last time, that *I* am Maxine Adler, and *I* am very much alive."

Click on the other end.

As tragic as it was to lose a human life, the passing of the *other* Maxine Adler did some good by benefiting our furry four-footed friends. Reportedly, in her will, *that* Maxine—who was a cat lover—bequeathed $7.6 million to the UC Davis School of Veterinary Medicine. The generous donation was earmarked for cancer research.

During the week that followed, the Adler Network phone lines lit up nonstop. People called to offer their sincerest condolences, only to discover that the Maxine they knew was not dead at all. On the upside, she found out that others truly cared about her.

Furthermore, for weeks after her non-death, Maxine and I expected a parade of widows from Woodfield Country Club, where she lived, to appear on her doorstep offering casseroles of brisket and noodle kugel to the grieving, lonely, and now eligible Owen Adler.

We were in stitches.

CHAPTER 26

Reality TV

BECAUSE I'M A SELF-PROCLAIMED *NEWS* junkie, I knew nothing about HGTV (Home & Garden Television) and the interest its reality shows were attracting since the time it launched back in 1994. It wasn't until Judy told me about it years later that I first heard about this new cable channel. She was *really* into it, spending hours watching HGTV shows in the evenings and over the weekend. Maybe it was because of the home furnishings course she had taken in college and her countless visits to builders' and developers' furnished model residences throughout her career. Those experiences gave her a voracious appetite for all things new and improved for the home.

That's also how I first became aware of HGTV's reality television series *Selling New York*, which premiered in the spring of 2010 and featured top real estate brokers and agents from three Manhattan-based real estate companies—Gumley Haft Kleier (which was later renamed Kleier Residential), CORE, and Warburg. Each of the firms sells New York luxury properties to cream-of-the-crop clientele.

The Adler Network succeeded in getting the One Thousand Ocean condominium building on the show—not once, but twice.

The One Thousand Ocean segments were with and *because of* the Kleiers: Michele Kleier, the brokerage company's co-president, and her daughters, Samantha Kleier-Forbes and Sabrina Kleier-Morgenstern, both executive vice presidents of the firm. They all were regulars on camera on that new series.

I instinctively reached out to Michele Kleier. I didn't know her, but I never felt intimidated making cold calls. It was my nature to be tenacious. The worst that could happen is that somebody would say no to my request or hang up. I could handle rejection.

Although the Kleiers weren't licensed to sell real estate in Florida and they told me so, I did think *something* good might come out of my phone call *if* Michele took the call. She did. I introduced myself and told her about One Thousand Ocean, which was under construction at the time. I believed that if the Kleiers could show the new property in an episode of *Selling New York*, it would provide tremendous exposure in front of prospective buyers. Millions of eyes would focus on the new project's ultra-luxe residences.

One Thousand Ocean buyers to date had originated mostly from the Northeast Corridor, which traditionally has been a strong feeder market to South Florida. Knowing that our client, LXR's Jamie Telchin, wanted to cultivate relationships with New York City brokers and their affluent clients, I saw an opportunity.

After Michele told me that she and her daughters planned to spend Thanksgiving week in Boca Raton where they own a downtown condominium, I arranged to meet them at the Boca Beach Club on one of those days. They would be sunbathing there.

So, off I went and met all three of these ladies in person. I enticed them—with Samantha and Sabrina's kids in tow—to visit One Thousand Ocean with me right then and there. It was located immediately adjacent to the Boca Beach Club. They agreed and were very impressed with what they saw. I also convinced them to stay on the property until Jamie arrived to speak to them. That's the beginning of how One Thousand Ocean became a reality TV star.

LXR and Gumley Haft Kleier soon entered into a strategic alliance. Both sides expected that alliance to result in referrals for one or more contracts for the designer-ready residences, penthouses, and beach villas, priced upward of more than $15 million.

The Kleiers frequently referred to Boca Raton as the sixth borough of New York. "It's an easy flight, and there are fabulous beaches, restaurants, shopping, and theaters," Michele told me. "A lot of people have family and close friends in Boca, so it's a great spot for Northeasterners to own a vacation property."

She confirmed what I already knew.

One Thousand Ocean was first filmed for *Selling New York* in 2010 when the building was under construction. That first segment aired during season one in May of 2010. Then in March 2011, LXR and the Kleiers hosted an evening for prominent New York brokers, agents, and prospects at the London Hotel in Manhattan's midtown area. The event, filmed for part of the second One Thousand Ocean segment, put the Boca Raton building into the spotlight. That evening, Jamie and his sales associates had an opportunity to introduce their property, show a video presentation, and meet with New York's most powerful brokers and agents. Celebrated guests such as Prince Lorenzo Borghese and Kelly Rutherford and Matthew Settle from the CW teen drama television series *Gossip Girl* added to the excitement.

The Kleiers were so impressed with One Thousand Ocean that they returned to the building and brought the *Selling New York* production crew back to Boca a few weeks later.

I can still remember what Samantha said as she explained the Kleiers' reaction when they visited One Thousand Ocean after it had been completed.

"Our mouths dropped open. In most units, everything is basically built out, including a refrigerator and freezer in the master closet in case you crave a glass of champagne or ice cream in the middle of the night. In addition, at One Thousand Ocean you not only have two parking spaces, but you also get an enclosed garage within the building. It really is one of the finest buildings in the country."

We worked with Meredith Lerner, a story producer with JV Productions, to coordinate the filming with the building staff. Along with showcasing several One Thousand Ocean residences and the neighboring Boca Raton Resort and Club (also an LXR property), the cameras followed local real estate brokers, buyers, and prospective buyers attending an elegant party held in the largest penthouse. More than three hundred stylish guests turned out to enjoy the "lights, camera, and action" and to meet the engaging and convivial Kleier family. We also succeeded in getting Venus Williams to attend. She was there to mingle with the upbeat crowd and be filmed. It was rumored that Venus and her interior design firm, V-Starr Interiors, would be furnishing a model residence in the building. That rumor turned out to be true. Of course, the Adler Network already knew about it.

We also threw in more exciting visuals, including female models from Bloomingdale's clad in designer spring fashions. And throughout the evening, the One Thousand Ocean sales associates gave tours of two furnished models, which showed the interior amenities and breathtaking views over the ocean, inlet, and Intracoastal.

A heaping bounty of lobster, crab claws, monster prawns, and other culinary selections had been expertly prepared by the Boca Raton Resort and Club's banquet department under the direction of George Petrocelli. This was displayed alongside a gigantic ice sculpture with the One Thousand Ocean logo etched into it. On both ends of the twenty-four-foot-long table stood two other huge blocks of ice sculpted in the shape of a fish.

During the evening, one of the massive (and heavy) ice sculptures crashed onto the floor. The sound was momentarily deafening. Gulping down an ocean-blue martini helped me take the edge off the surprising descent. Fortunately, the attentive catering staff was quick to avert what could have been injuries—or a flood.

We encountered another glitch that evening. *Boca Raton Magazine* Editor Kevin Kaminski became locked in one of the restrooms. We didn't want this to happen to *anyone*, and especially not to the editor of the city magazine! But Kevin was a good sport about it, and we continued laughing about the incident long after it had occurred.

That event attracted a lot of press. We even sent film footage to *Access Hollywood*, and the TV entertainment news program aired a portion of it.

Together, the filming at the London Hotel, the Boca Raton Resort and Club, and One Thousand Ocean aired as a segment in a *Selling New York* episode during the show's third season in August 2011. Because this was the second time that One Thousand Ocean had been featured on the series, it was a double hit for us. And we had doubled the pleasure for a client.

To mark One Thousand Ocean's starring role in the second segment on *Selling New York*, we held a Private Prescreening event—again in the building's largest penthouse. This exclusive gathering took place on the same evening that the episode was scheduled to air on HGTV. Hosted by LXR, this event enabled partygoers to preview the episode before others across the United States and Canada saw it. Sabrina Kleier-Morgenstern was the celebrity guest of honor. She was a welcomed addition to the festivities, which included a cocktail and dessert receptions replete with movie concession-type treats, as well as the prescreening on a giant screen. Michele and Samantha had planned to attend too, but at the last minute they had to remain in New York to film another episode in the popular series. As they say in the entertainment world, the show must go on.

Also, in the fall of 2011, we planned another event featuring the Kleiers at One Thousand Ocean. They had just had their novel, *Hot Property*, published by Harper Collins, so we staged a cocktail reception and book signing in the penthouse that promoted the book as well as One Thousand Ocean. Books were given out to guests—compliments of the developer.

The book is fiction, but *Hot Property* is based on the Kleiers' real-life adventures as high-flying brokers for the Manhattan elite. This roman á clef gives readers a glance inside some of the New York City's most expensive residences, as well as a peek into the lives of their wealthy owners. Judy and I loved it, and we both agreed we should have been in real estate sales. But it hadn't been in the cards for us. We were doing the next best thing: *promoting the sale* of upscale real estate properties.

That book-signing reception was reserved only for One Thousand Ocean residents, serious potential buyers, and top real estate professionals from the area. Miss Florida USA, Karina Brez, attended and posed for photographs along with the Kleiers. Karina was a beautiful, poised young woman who provided an additional enhancement, although one wasn't needed. The delightfully delicious Kleiers were magnetic in their own right.

Judy and I have spent a lot of time with the Kleier ladies, who comprise the most dynamic and close-knit mother-and-daughters team we have ever come across. They are smart, personable, and passionate. They are always busy, surrounded by a whirlwind of work and family activities. You can put your finger on the energy around them. No wonder they have been so successful in their field—and on reality television.

No outside Florida brokers ever had exclusivity to sell the new condominiums at One Thousand Ocean, yet they brought buyers there and co-brokered many of the sales. And even though the Kleiers had let us know umpteen times that they weren't licensed to sell real estate in Florida, their alliance with LXR generated several referrals of qualified buyers seeking a one-of-a-kind oceanfront residence. And there was an immediate sale.

But the best part of all for us is that we developed an ongoing relationship with the wonderful, highly entertaining, and lovable Kleier family. As you can see from the foreword in this book, the admiration is mutual. What originally began as a relationship on behalf of a client grew into a very special friendship, which I truly cherish.

CHAPTER 27

Venus, If You Will

THE VENUS WHO I CAME to know is the famed tennis champion *off* the court: a talented designer, and a grounded and unpretentious individual with a giant heart. The Adler Network was truly blessed to have forged a relationship with her beginning in 2004.

In chapter 20, you learned of Venus Williams's support of the "I Have a Dream" Foundation, an organization that encourages and rewards at-risk kids to stay in school, stay out of trouble, and graduate high school. They are rewarded with a college or vocational school education by their sponsors.

But there's much more to tell.

V-STARR MODEL RESIDENCE

Because not every prospective condominium or home buyer possesses vision, it's beneficial for real estate developers or builders to create furnished models where visitors can see the potential of the spaces and how they function best. Certainly, having a signature design by a celebrity also helps to attract a much larger market of prospects.

That's the reason I once again reached out to Venus. She had established her own interior design firm in 2002—V-Starr Interiors based in Jupiter, Florida. We felt that her international brand coupled with the high-end brand we had crafted for the One Thousand Ocean condominium in Boca Raton would be a perfect match.

After introducing Venus to Jamie Telchin, they both agreed. One Thousand Ocean's marketing team worked closely with Venus and Sonya Haffey, V-Starr Interiors' director of design, to create a furnished model residence at the new property.

The four-bedroom, four-and-one-half bath model, listed for $6.45 million, opened in March 2012 at an event for more than three hundred guests. Sister Serena Williams was on hand that night to see Venus's talents being showcased. With both celebrated tennis stars present, the media were in full force. We also remember how interested Venus had been to find out her kid sister's opinion of the design. It was obvious to us that Serena was a very important part of her life.

The model residence had exquisite exposures to the southeast, overlooking both the Atlantic shoreline and the Intracoastal Waterway. Venus and her design staff had brought the outside in by incorporating a lot of ice and sea blue colors. It felt "beachy" while still being elegant.

Prior to the model opening, Venus had made several visits to One Thousand Ocean. She never arrived with an entourage. She either drove alone in her SUV or was accompanied by Jessica Baron, her executive assistant. Jessica had been very helpful to us by giving us Venus's tournament schedule and setting up dates when Venus could be available for meetings and events.

Several days before this event, we held a press conference so that the media could walk through the residence and then ask Venus questions. She was as gracious as one could possibly be. Venus is always a draw, so we were assured of a great turnout.

For those who have only seen Venus on the tennis court (either in person or on television), let us tell you something else. With full makeup and her hair styled professionally, she looked absolutely amazing! And I was very flattered when Venus entrusted me to hold her purse while she was being interviewed and photographed.

In the fall of 2012, we were able to get a cover story about this model residence in the highly regarded *Florida Design* magazine. For the first time in its publishing history, the magazine featured a "cover girl" on the front cover, along with a residential interior photograph related to the inside story. That cover girl was Venus Williams.

Once again, I was amazed that Maxine had been able to pull this off. I suspect it was because of her salesmanship abilities and her longstanding relationship with the publisher.

In an Adler Network news release announcing the upcoming issue of the magazine, Jeff Lichtenstein said, "We have never put anyone on our front cover before. However, in this particular instance, our focus is on two icons, and we felt they both deserve top billing—one being Williams and the other an iconic building in a world-class city."

Once again, a valued colleague had made us look good.

Extreme Furniture Makeover

In 2014 I was successful in pairing Venus Williams with global home furnishings retailer Roche Bobois. This occurred after Venus told us about the Sundari Foundation's Lotus House. At that time, Roche Bobois's locations in Florida included Coral Gables and North Miami Beach. (Later, this client of ours opened a showroom in Aventura).

A year earlier, Roche Bobois had donated new furniture valued at $700,000 to Kristi House, the designated advocacy center for child victims of sexual abuse and exploitation in Miami-Dade County. Now Roche Bobois's Julien Bigan was pleased to make a similar donation of furnishings to Lotus House.

The Miami-based Lotus House shelter and life skills resource center for homeless and abused women was among Venus's pet charities. It was in need of new furniture, which Roche Bobois subsequently donated. Items included dozens of new sofas, chairs, tables, sideboards, desks, bedroom and dining furniture, and accessories. Then about a week after the furnishings were installed, Venus toured the center and shared some encouraging words with its residents. Much of what she said reflected valuable lessons she had learned from her mother, Oracene Price. Her mother was with Venus on that day, and I was delighted to meet her.

Venus's words made a powerful impact. "One of the most important lessons my mother taught me was to be confident and believe in myself. That really resonated with me because it's not always easy to be successful, and it's even harder on you when you fail. That's going to happen too. You're going to fail. But that doesn't mean it's the end. When you fail, it means you're at least trying something, which shows you're on the right path."

Lotus House strives to make its residents feel safe and cared for so that they can begin the process of healing and reclaiming their lives. Programs assist residents in improving their interpersonal and work skills to help them become productive and self-sufficient when they are ready to leave. We all hoped that, with these beautiful new furnishings, residents would have a greater sense of self-worth and feel more positive about the future.

There's still more.

Three months later, at a fundraiser at a gallery in Miami's Wynwood Arts District, Lotus House honored Venus, V-Starr Interiors, and Roche Bobois's Julien Bigan for their charitable efforts. They received a certificate of appreciation for their Extreme Furniture Makeover at the shelter.

It warmed my heart—and Venus's heart—to see that partnership net favorable results for women and children in need.

Venus's Biggest Challenge

After withdrawing from the US Open in September 2011, Venus disclosed to the world that she had been diagnosed with Sjogren's syndrome, a debilitating, chronic autoimmune disorder that causes very low energy levels, joint pain, dry eyes and mouth, and other uncomfortable symptoms.

I think that this illness may have become the biggest challenge in her life, but she refused to accept defeat. Instead, Venus took a short hiatus from her competitive tennis schedule while changing her diet and exercise regime. She needed time to adjust.

We were in Venus's company frequently during that time, which coincided with plans for V-Starr Interiors' model residence at One Thousand Ocean. She was open with us about the challenge she faced in light of the disorder, which had taken years for her doctors to diagnose. Discovering what was wrong with her didn't lessen her ambition or enthusiasm. She seemed to be relieved after she finally knew what was wrong with her.

More than four million people in the United States are reportedly inflicted with the illness; most of them are females. There is a need for education, and Venus recognized that need and rose to the occasion.

Since then, Venus has modified her life to live with Sjogren's syndrome. There are treatments but no cure to date. She still heads V-Starr Interiors, relaunched her EleVen active-wear line, and plays competitively on the professional worldwide tennis circuit while watching her younger sister Serena outperform her own sports career. Knowing Venus like I do, my guess is that she continues to be Serena's greatest cheerleader and fan.

Venus Williams could spend all of her time in ways that financially enrich her multiple careers. But *this* shining superstar has proven time and time again to be a woman of valor who reaches out and helps others without expecting anything in return. For her, unconditional giving seems to always be an *ace*.

CHAPTER 28

At the Movies

I T'S NOT EVERY DAY THAT a public relations client gets to appear in a Hollywood movie. But One Thousand Ocean did.

In 2011, a film crew from Flashfire Productions spent an entire Sunday at the ocean-to-Intracoastal condominium building in Boca Raton. They were shooting a key scene with actors Jennifer Lopez and Jason Statham for the action-thriller *Parker*. It took place in One Thousand Ocean's Signature Penthouse 601, a new residence that was available for purchase.

Adapted from the novel *Flashfire* by author Donald Westlake, the film depicted JLo as a real estate agent involved with a thief (Statham), who was planning a heist at a Palm Beach auction. The production crew and director Taylor Hackford (e.g., *Officer and a Gentleman*, the biopic *Ray*) had singled out One Thousand Ocean for the on-location shoot after scouting several other sites. My guess is they made that choice because the building is a truly unique and highly prestigious property.

The developer's representative, Jamie Telchin, learned about the movie plot and then granted them permission to film the scenes.

I first received a call from Jamie about this on a weekend. My agency was called upon to immediately coordinate the shoot between the production company, the film crew, and the One Thousand Ocean building staff.

The behind-the-scenes action was as interesting as the filming itself, as the actors prepared for their roles and camera crews moved around the driveway leading to the entrance of One Thousand Ocean. The crew literally took over the building. Jamie was on hand, and the building's staff went to great lengths to make sure everything ran smoothly. In spite of the extra work it required, he—and we—agreed it was worth it.

During the filming, paparazzi were camped out nearby. When ABC television affiliate WPBF got wind of what was occurring, their newscast mentioned the film shoot at a "secret location in Boca Raton." This generated a lot of curiosity, along with more publicity.

You can be sure we milked it by sending out our own press release that disclosed One Thousand Ocean as that "secret location."

Just days later, the crew shot another scene adjacent to the One Thousand Ocean sales center (located diagonally across the street, overlooking Lake Boca Raton). They also shot in the Boca Raton Resort and Club's Cloister lobby and at its landmark Pink Tower.

To celebrate the nationwide premiere of *Parker* in late January 2013, we coordinated a Private Screening party for One Thousand Ocean special guests (new residents, Boca Raton Mayor Susan Whelchel, other area VIPs, the marketing team, and Randi Emerman, president of the Palm Beach International Film Festival). We reserved seats on the Premier Theater level at the Cinemark Palace Twenty in Boca Raton, and every guest received complimentary valet parking, a movie ticket, and popcorn. It was very exciting to see the building on the big screen, as well as having its name mentioned. While JLo and Jason Statham may have had top billing, the guests viewing the film considered the real stars to be the cityscapes of West Palm Beach and the Island of Palm Beach—and, of course, One Thousand Ocean and the Boca Raton Resort! All of us whistled and applauded with pride during the scenes that had been filmed there.

Likewise, the mayor was thrilled because the local economy gets a boost whenever filmmakers come to the area. They create local jobs, use local services, book hotel rooms, and patronize restaurants.

A dessert reception followed the special screening in the Screen Writer's Room at Bogart's Bar and Grill, marking a role well played.

CHAPTER 29

Shorts

He Left His "Marc"

Aside from Judy, the employee with the longest tenure at the Adler Network was Marc Streeter. He was our creative director when the agency offered advertising services, as well as a PR account supervisor, writer, and event planner. Marc had a great sense of humor and the voice of a broadcaster. For years, even after he left my firm, his taped voice encouraged callers to leave their voice-mail messages on our phone lines.

One day, I asked our receptionist Tracy to place a call to China in order to obtain a copy of a magazine that was published there. Neither Tracy nor any of us spoke Mandarin. Along with the difference in time zones, this was quite a challenge. Luckily, the person answering the phone in Shanghai spoke some broken English and eventually was able to comprehend Tracy's request.

Before Tracy hung up, all of us could hear Marc's booming voice in the background.

"Tell her to also send an order of subgum chow mein…and not to forget the chopsticks."

This was quite a mouthful for Tracy to digest. Meanwhile, the rest of us couldn't catch our breaths from laughing.

No. She didn't place the food order.

CHILI CON CARNE

Judy, Marc, and I were sitting in the Adler Network conference room in Fort Lauderdale. It had a large round glass-top table that doubled as a dining table when we expected clients or members of the media to join us for lunch.

I had made a lunch appointment with a prospective new client, and we were awaiting his arrival. He said he was starting up a business as a private chef in people's homes and wanted us to create awareness of his service. He also had told me he would be bringing in lunch for us, so we were salivating in anticipation of his gourmet goodies.

Although the chef delivered on his promise, it was not quite as we had expected.

Our agency's conference room had large picture windows at the front of the building, and we were watching for our guest to arrive. What we saw was a middle-aged man, wearing a white apron, carrying a huge pot across the parking lot. Suddenly, the pot fell, tossing all of its thick, soupy, brown contents onto the asphalt. I'm sure I don't have to tell you what it looked like! Nevertheless, he calmly scooped up the slop with a large ladle and put it back into the pot.

We were beside ourselves in hysterics but were able to agree that there was no way any of us would put that food, whatever it was, into our mouths.

When the chef entered our office, we greeted him. I don't know how we had regained our composure. He apologized for the dark brown stains on his apron. Then he insisted we sit down right away so he could serve us his gourmet chili while it was still hot.

We made excuses and didn't eat it. We also dissuaded him from hiring us. Furthermore, to this day, whenever I see someone eating chili con carne, I flinch.

You just can't make this stuff up.

Beyond the Hundred-Yard Line

When the Adler Network was representing Indiana-based Dutch Made Custom Cabinetry during the early nineties, the company signed a barter contract with Dan Marino. Dutch Made provided its high-quality cabinetry for the home of the Miami Dolphins quarterback and his wife Claire in Windmill Ranches in Weston, Florida. In return, Dutch Made was granted the use of Dan's name and testimonial about the cabinetry in its marketing for a period of about two years.

I made several visits to the Marino residence after the cabinets had been installed in their kitchen, pub room, and elsewhere. As I pulled into their driveway, I remember seeing a lot of clay flower pots filled with colorful impatiens. I had similar pots with impatiens on the patio in my own home. I loved them. They were very welcoming.

Claire was always present during my visits, and I found her to be friendly and warm to talk to. We had the cabinetry photographed for use in Dutch Made ads and for publicity (we handled the latter).

Coincidentally (if there really *are* coincidences), the Adler Network had just hired a writer from the *Miami Herald.* A week before she started working for us, she had written and filed a story about autism, and she had interviewed the Marinos about their autistic child. In 1992, the Marinos had established the Dan Marino Foundation to improve the lives of people with autism and other special needs.

On a lighter note, here's a side story about the aforementioned football player.

Owen and I frequently ate at Mario the Baker in Sunrise, a popular restaurant located just a few minutes from where we lived in Plantation. We were friendly with Henry Olmino, the owner and chef. After Henry opened a second restaurant, Mario's East on Las Olas Boulevard in Fort Lauderdale, we dined there one evening with another couple. Dan and a bunch of his buddies were seated at the table adjacent to ours. When our check arrived, Owen reached over and handed it to Dan. He asked him to autograph it. Dan began to sign but quickly realized he would be signing *our* check. All of us, including Dan, broke into laughter. That was *so* Owen Adler!

DON'T SWEAT THE SMALL STUFF

Back in 1998 when we were working with Boca Developers, we planned a special evening at the new Townsend Place condominium community in downtown Boca Raton. It headlined psychologist and self-help author Dr. Richard Carlson. *People* magazine had named him one of the most intriguing personalities a year before, so we knew he would be a big draw for this event. Dr. Carlson had gained fame from his best-selling books, one of which was *Don't Sweat the Small Stuff*, published in 1997. It became one of the fastest-selling books of all time and was on the New York Times Best Seller list for over one hundred weeks.

His prescription for a calmer, more enjoyable and meaningful life was concurrent with Boca Developers' vision of creating easy lifestyles. "When we sweat the small stuff," the expert noted, "we lose touch with the magic and beauty around us." Because those developers fashioned communities that were helpful in maintaining that magic and beauty, they were happy to have Dr. Carlson speak in a location that reflected their philosophy.

We had arranged for the developers to buy copies of *Don't Sweat the Small Stuff* in advance, so guests found a complimentary book on their seats when they arrived. Dr. Carlson later autographed them. Several guests had previously purchased his book and brought it with them that evening. They couldn't wait to meet our guest speaker in person.

I also arranged for Dr. Carlson to stay overnight at the Aragon oceanfront condominium, another of Boca Developers' properties. He told me that looking out over the ocean had boosted his creativity as he worked on another book.

Judy had set up press interviews with Dr. Carlson every half an hour, which occurred earlier on the day of the event. She was the gatekeeper, so to speak, who tried keeping Dr. Carlson on schedule. Everything went along smoothly until Rod Stafford Hagwood of the *Sun-Sentinel* arrived. She had to keep him waiting about fifteen minutes. The following day, in a blurb Rod wrote on the inside front cover of the newspaper's main section, he referred to Boca Developers' "publicist" in disparaging terms. (Hey, Rod, Judy was just doing her job.) We can't recall his exact words, nor do we want to!

By 2003, however, I guess Rod had forgiven me because he provided great press coverage of the WCI/Neiman Marcus Bal Harbour fashion show event we were involved in.

PUBLICITY HOUND

As some news networks disclosed during the 2016 US presidential campaigns, Donald Trump sometimes used "John Barron" or "John Miller" instead of his real name earlier in his career. Trump reportedly had masqueraded as a PR spokesperson for himself when reaching out to the media to share information and try to get publicity. But that wasn't always the case. He also gave his true identity, and I was a witness to that.

I was in a meeting with Adam Goodkin, the publisher of South Florida's *Simply the Best* magazine, when a call came in for Adam from "Donald Trump." There had been speculation that the real estate tycoon might make a presidential run back in 2000.

Adam took the call and listened intently. He then walked over to me, put his hand over the phone's mouthpiece and repeated what Trump had told him. Trump was indeed thinking of running for the presidential nomination and wanted *Simply the Best* to put him on the front cover. He told Adam he'd allow it if the magazine would write an article about him.

"What should I say?" Adam asked me.

"Say yes," I told him. No matter what I personally thought of Mr. Trump, he was a magnet and would undoubtedly increase readership of Adam's magazine, which was relatively new at the time.

You would think that a hard-working, wealthy man like Donald Trump would have hired a public relations firm to get publicity for him. Perhaps he had done so. But he obviously preferred to be hands on when dealing with some of the media. He liked direct contact. In my opinion, he also is the perfect person to associate with the epigraph at the beginning of this book: "There is only one thing in the world worse than being talked about, and that is not being talked about."

Or in the words of my dear father, Herman Schwartz, who tried to console me after someone had called me names during my childhood: "Talk about me good. Talk about me bad. But just talk about me!"

HILLARY

In 2001 our agency came up with a Designer/Penthouse Program for Acqualina Ocean Residences and Resort in Sunny Isles Beach. After speaking with the editor of *Architectural Digest*, who helped us determine the nation's foremost interior design firms, I selected and reached out to some of them. The purpose was to invite them to present creative concepts for an assigned penthouse floor plan in the world-class building. Still under construction, these penthouses were veritable "mansions in the sky." If a prospective purchaser bought the penthouse and liked the designer's vision, that designer would likely get the commission to do the job on the interior of the unit.

One of those firms, Brown Davis Interiors, had its headquarters in the nation's capital. The company had done a lot of impressive design work, including commissions for former President Bill Clinton and Senator Hillary Rodham Clinton's Washington, DC, and Chappaqua, New York, residences.

I became friends with Todd Davis and Robert Brown. Every time I spoke to Todd on the phone when he was in DC, he'd ask how the weather was in Florida. We'd make the comparison—and before you know it, he and Rob decided to open a second office, in Miami.

Beyond thrilled, I accepted their invitation to attend a reception they would be hosting for Senator Hillary Clinton in the fall of 2001. It was being held in their historic Georgetown residence, which had been written up in *Architectural Digest* and other magazines. Hillary was going to be honored, and I was a fan of hers. I also had never been inside of a Georgetown townhome before and looked forward to seeing one—even more so because Todd and Rob owned the one where the event was taking place.

Owen and I flew to Washington, DC, along with Michael Goldstein, vice president of sales and marketing for Acqualina. Michael had made a name for himself in South Florida real estate, first with the Sunshine Group (Florida) and at the present time with the Trump Group. He had come a long way from driving a taxi cab in New York in his younger years! This just goes to show you that *anything* is possible, if you work hard, pay your dues, and are in the right place at the right time.

The interiors of the historic townhome were stunning, with a lot of character and detail. I also remember the small yet enchanting rear outdoor area with its magnificent foliage.

On the evening that we met Hillary, former President Bill Clinton wasn't there. She was, however, joined by her mother, Dorothy Howell Rodham. It was an amazing experience for me to see Hillary relaxed, surrounded by admirers, and supporters. I was a fly on the wall as I watched guests throw a wide range of questions out to her, from the arts to health care and just about every subject in between. She answered naturally, knowledgeably, and spontaneously, without being scripted. She also carried herself with grace, and I found her to be down to earth. I kept remarking to Owen and Michael that she was the smartest woman I had ever met in my life.

When it got to be around eleven o'clock, the three of us decided to go have dinner. We only had consumed drinks and hors d'oeuvres. Although they were bountiful, our appetites were really kicking in. Following Todd and Rob's recommendation of a nearby restaurant, we set out on foot through the main area of Georgetown. As we looked toward the White House, there was a huge fireworks display coloring the sky. It marked the conclusion of a state dinner that President George W. Bush and First Lady Laura Bush were hosting that evening during their first administration. The guests of honor were Mexican President Vicente Fox and Mexico's First Lady Martha Sahagun de Fox.

Earlier in the day, I had heard that this dinner would be taking place. So there we were, witnesses to how the White House entertained special dignitaries. Owen and Michael kept looking at me as tear drops rolled down my cheeks. As I told you before, I turn on the waterworks when it comes to patriotism. At that moment, I felt that only in America could we be so blessed to see events such as this one take place. I certainly was proud, and it showed on my tear-soaked sleeve.

That was just seven days before the atrocious acts of 9/11 would shake our nation but not defeat it.

CONCRETE FACTS

It was very early on a Saturday morning in 2002 when Judy was the only car driving east on the William Lehman Causeway en route to the construction site for the Acqualina Ocean Residences and Resort in Sunny Isles Beach. She was surrounded by at least two dozen Tarmac concrete trucks. It was a very strange and surreal experience, like something out of a sci-fi flick. There she was, alone with those large trucks, in her modest midsized Japanese import.

This was the day that one hundred forty five concrete trucks lined up along Collins Avenue to pour concrete for the foundation of the fifty-one-story Acqualina tower. The process took fifteen hours to pour the estimated nine thousand nine hundred twenty cubic yards of concrete. This was the largest "mat foundation pour" in all of South Florida to date.

Judy told me she became very emotional and misty-eyed. It was as if she was giving birth to a baby. That baby was going to be the tallest residential high-rise hotel and condominium along the entire eastern US coastline, and it would soar above four hundred feet of Atlantic shoreline.

Michael Goldstein had invited buyers, prospects, and local government VIPs to watch the construction activity. We invited the media. Along with observing the pouring of this foundation, guests enjoyed an outpour of mimosas that accompanied breakfast and lunch fare, compliments of the developer, the Trump Group. The dramatic action had begun at 3:00 a.m. and continued until 5:00 p.m.

We continued to tout the towering height of the sky-high Acqualina until the attacks on the World Trade Center's twin towers on 9/11. Following those dreadful events, we no longer brought attention to the building's height.

It is important to be aware of current world events and adjust PR strategies accordingly. You cannot remain insular and not know what is happening around you.

DEADBEATS

We had more than our fair share of deadbeat clients who didn't pay their bills in full over the years. On one occasion, we took three clients to court after having hired a new attorney to represent us. At the same time, out of the goodness of our hearts, we hired the attorney's daughter, a newbie to our industry. She was not an asset. But we *did* win our cases, and the funds were being held in our attorney's escrow account. Before we could get our money out, he absconded with all of it and eventually was disbarred from practicing law. We lost a sizable amount of money. I think this was probably meant to be because despite my dear and disgruntled husband's wishes, I sometimes kept working for clients even when they were in arrears. My bad!

TURTLES

Before LXR Luxury Resorts began to develop the private peninsula where One Thousand Ocean would rise, the company knew that paying attention to every last detail would be paramount in the permitting process. That included addressing environmental concerns such as preserving the sea-turtle-nesting beach that bordered the site. This was done through a significant dune restoration in addition to complying with federal, state, and city turtle-friendly lighting regulations. Even though we were aware of sea turtles for a long time from having worked with other developers of oceanfront properties, this was the first time we truly were *educated* about them.

We learned that loggerhead, green, and leatherback turtles swim ashore to lay eggs and produce hatchlings between March 1 and October 31 and that southeast Florida was the second largest nesting site for loggerheads in the world. The sea turtle populations, however, have declined and have become a threatened species. Therefore, steps must be taken to stop the decline, or they could become extinct.

A consulting firm for One Thousand Ocean proactively scheduled meetings with the Department of Environmental Protection and the Florida Fish and Wildlife Conservation Commission in order to collectively develop an appropriate turtle-safe lighting plan for the new building. LXR invited agency representatives out to the site prior to the final inspection to ensure that the lights installed to date were compliant. As work progressed, LXR continued to interact with those agencies. The company also worked with the city because of its own turtle ordinances. We discovered that in 1986, Boca Raton had been one of the first municipalities within the state to enact a turtle lighting ordinance.

One Thousand Ocean's healthy dune system was a good natural buffer for storms. Aside from providing a sand bank to help combat erosion, the dunes would serve as a landward boundary for the turtles, keeping them in their natural beach habitat. These dunes also would help block artificial lights at ground level that disorient these marine creatures. Hatchlings instinctively navigate themselves toward the light on the horizon. If light comes from a source other than the moon over the ocean, the turtles become confused and don't know where to go. They will die if they remain on the beach for too long since they need water to survive.

All of this information was important when we planned events at the building. It also made for great coffee-table talk!

THE EENSY-WEENSY SPIDER

When my kids and grandkids were small, instead of humming lullabies to them, I sang and demonstrated the Eensy-Weensy Spider going up the water spout. I now have the joy of doing the same thing with my great grandchildren. How wonderful is that?

One evening many years ago, Owen and I were watching a television special. Barbra Streisand and her son Jason Gould were the featured guests. Babs had given birth to Jason while she was married to actor Elliot Gould.

During the interview, the show's host asked Jason if his mother had sung him either traditional lullabies or some of her hit songs to put him to sleep.

"Neither," he answered. "She sang 'The Eensy-Weensy Spider' to me."

I *kvelled* with pride.

Humpty Dumpty

Because we represented numerous developers and builders, we were always going onto their construction sites.

Judy and I both thought of ourselves as poised and certainly not klutzes. But that changed when the One Thousand Ocean condominium was under construction. Oftentimes the entire marketing team would do a "walk through" of the building. There usually was a group of eight or more of us.

Judy and I always wore high heels on visits such as this. This was just a habit and the desire to keep our appearance "professional" at all times. (We also never went without stockings.) On two occasions, Judy got her heels caught on a wood floor plank and toppled over. She nearly died of embarrassment as our client fussed over her to ensure she hadn't been injured. She wasn't hurt—but, boy, was she red in the face!

Then it was *my* turn.

About a year later, after One Thousand Ocean had been completed, I was in one of the penthouses with the president of development when I lost my balance, fell back, and hit my head on a credenza. All hell broke loose! The building staff immediately appeared with a tub of ice. Fortunately, I was okay.

Then on another occasion, I was attending a grand opening party in a model home at one of Toll Brothers' new communities. It was beautifully furnished and as clean as a whistle—*so* clean that I almost walked through a plate-glass sliding door. The sound of my head striking the glass panel caused heads to turn. The following week, aside from having a large bump on my head, I was inundated with calls from Toll Brothers' managers. Toll Brothers was a large public company, and I'm sure they didn't want a lawsuit. That, however, was never a thought of mine.

In both of these cases, I could definitely relate to the embarrassment Judy had felt. Thankfully, there had been no serious bodily injuries.

Maybe we *were* klutzes after all.

CRACK

On a somewhat related note, throughout my career I never took a sick day. I ate relatively healthy, exercised early every morning, and had regular checkups. I simply never became ill. That's what makes the following tale so significant.

Judy's boyfriend Doug Black came to several of the events that we held for our clients, and once he attended a family gathering. Although he is physically strong and oftentimes epitomizes the Alpha male, he is very warm and affectionate. As soon as he saw me, he rushed over to say hello. He literally lifted me off the ground and gave me a big bear hug.

Crack.

Yep. Doug fractured several of my ribs.

Feeling terribly guilty about what he had done, the following day he took time off from his work, bought an orchid plant for me, and personally delivered it to my office. But I was at another office—a doctor's office getting x-rayed.

Doug hoped that the orchid plant would last longer than my lingering pain did.

To this day, Judy ribs Doug about the incident and warns him not to do this to *her*. Or to me *again*.

JUDY-ISMS

I am a Virgo. True to my astrological sun sign, I will do anything for the people I love. I am also gutsy and determined to do whatever it takes to get what I want. And while I've gotten most of what I've wanted over the years—especially the really important things like *love, family,* and *dear friends*, I didn't always get the reaction or performance I had expected from people in a particular situation. And at times, I didn't get some of the clients I would have liked to have represented.

Like most Virgos, I am also analytical—probably more analytical than most people who share my sign. I can analyze something to death! I used to do that a lot at the office. That's when Judy stepped in with one of her Judy-isms.

"What *is*, *is*, Maxine."

Although not always original, words such as these helped me to stop dwelling on things that were beyond my control. They moved me forward ho! I am glad that Judy was there to steer me in the right direction.

CHOP-CHOP

When Judy and I arrived at Williams Island in Aventura in 2000 to interview one of the community's newest celebrity residents, Jorge Chavez, the first thing the native Peruvian jockey directed my way was a question.

"How much do you weigh, Maxine?"

Sure, I was petite and lean, but no one had ever asked me my weight before except for my doctors. Nicknamed "Chop-Chop" because of his whipping style when he raced, Chavez had competed in the Kentucky Derby and won two Breeders' Cup races. We subsequently got coverage in the *Wall Street Journal* about him buying a condominium at Williams Island.

But it was his peculiar question, which apparently wasn't peculiar for a jockey to ask, that I will always remember.

HARPER'S "BIZARRE"

Another question was posed to me that I also thought was a bit bizarre. In 2015, I was in New York City celebrating the reopening of the recently revamped Roche Bobois home furnishings showroom on Madison Avenue. Many of the company's VIPs attended, including those who had flown in from France for the event.

Fashion and home furnishings always have gone hand in hand, so *Harper's Bazaar* was a partner with Roche Bobois on that evening. I was dressed in a two-piece black cocktail dress that had been custom designed for me by South Florida designer Craig Signer. The off-the-shoulder top was made of matte jersey with satin cuffs and trim around the shoulders. The matte jersey mid-calf skirt had a dramatic satin flounce. It was very distinctive looking and a Signer original design.

As I was "working the room" as I always did, I made my way over to the entrance of the showroom where *Harper's Bazaar* had staged a logo backdrop. As guests arrived, they were photographed.

I introduced myself to an editor from the esteemed magazine, who then asked, "*Who* are you wearing?"

At times in my past, I'd been asked *where* I had purchased a particular item of clothing, but never *who* made it. I suppose in New York or Los Angeles, and in the fashion industry, that is a very normal inquiry. For a fleeting moment, I felt as if I was standing on a Hollywood red carpet, being scrutinized *or* complimented by the fashion police!

CHAPTER 30

Introspection

"JUDY! CAN YOU GET MAXINE to come over here…now? It's time to leave. We've been here since the crack of dawn. It's enough already," Owen said. Like always, he was getting annoyed because Maxine continued to play her Perle Mesta role even after the party had ended.

"I'll try, Owen, but you know how she is," I replied, walking away from him and toward Maxine who was engaged in conversation with some of the remaining guests.

"Excuse me for interrupting. Maxine, Owen needs you. Can you go talk to him, please? Now?"

This was so-o-o Maxine. I always had to drag her away from doing what she did best and that was being the perfect PR professional. Personable. Passionate. Giving everything she had. Taking no shortcuts. Absolutely tireless.

After another five minutes or so, she finally broke away and returned to our group. We were waiting in the designated media area close to the inlet. Bernadette Chevannes, our wonderful longtime receptionist, was trying to salvage our media signs and registration sheets that were now covered in the same layer of gray dust that enveloped our clothing and shoes. By now, we all had shed our surgical masks.

"Okay, everyone. I'm here!" I announced. "Let's call it a day. Congratulations on a great job working with the media and doing everything you could to take care of them. See you all back in the office tomorrow morning."

Owen had already started walking toward the parking lot. I was anticipating his irritation when he saw his car. Maxine and I quickly caught up with him.

"Be nice," I whispered to her. I didn't have to say that, because Maxine always was nice to her husband. And even when Owen got annoyed with Maxine, he too was respectful of her. They were an amazing couple. The perfect couple. I based that assessment on the eight years I had been working with them so far. I was involved in both their professional and personal lives.

After spotting all of the parked cars covered in the same thick sheet of dust, it was easy to imagine this being the result of a war, a terror attack, or a natural disaster. But it wasn't. It was simply the aftermath of the implosion of the Harbour House North apartment building in Bal Harbour, Florida. And we couldn't have been more pleased with the outcome or that we had been among the key players.

But as I had predicted, Owen was displeased over the condition of his black Lexus. The three of us got inside, and he started the drive back to Boca Raton. He made one stop first. It was at a car wash. Owen always kept the Adlers' jet-black cars so sparkling clean that you could see your reflection bouncing off the surface.

Meanwhile, I could tell that Maxine was thinking. She was always thinking. And she was smiling too. I could easily get inside of her head, so I knew she was expressing silent gratitude, not only for having been involved with this event—but for being able to be involved in life, *in ways she never had imagined.*

Most of us have one person or one occurrence in our early years that inspires us toward a goal. Initially, I wanted to work in the mental health field, but I had been told I'd become too attached and that I wouldn't leave my patients' problems at the office; I would bring my involvement home with me because I was the kind of person who cared too much. So I was diverted into marketing and public relations instead. But I must tell you: I cared just as much about my *clients* as I would have cared about my *patients*. I rarely slept because I was driven to create opportunities for them in order to get them the positive exposure they were paying me to deliver. I also worked hard to come up with solutions to their challenges and problems. Either way, I'd like to think that I made a small difference, left a lasting impression, and helped a lot of people—even if my primary focus was PR in the real estate and design fields, not in health care.

Although I believe that things are meant to be, it wasn't until my later years that I came to realize and accept that I couldn't control it all. When I finally let go, I saw my life more clearly. It was as if that colossal cloud of gray dust had disappeared. It made it easier for me to walk along my path—not the one that *I* had chosen, but the path that had chosen *me*.

AFTERWORD

THE OBJECTIVE OF THIS BOOK was to provide an insider's view into the lives of public relations professionals and their clients during the time when skill, face-to-face communications, and special relationships were what counted most. As PR continues to evolve, technology has been pushed to the forefront. With the ability to present your message instantaneously on the Internet, the press release as well as printed publications may soon go by the wayside. So be it. Who am I to question or stop progress? Yet I still prefer things the way they were when Judy and I practiced the profession. We left our marks before waves of electronic and digital innovation rolled in, and I think there is a lot to be said for *and* learned from the old ways. While a one hundred forty-character tweet or posting a YouTube video may briefly inform, alter public opinion (or give false news!), and reach millions of people, this is simply not the same as providing full and accurate information to your target audience.

My passion for public relations continues to this day. And fortunately I am able to revisit these and many other stories anytime I want to. I backtrack in my mind, and they all come rushing forth—all of the glamour, the construction dirt, the deadlines, the dedication, and the long hours. For our team, PR was a highly personalized and demanding business. Nevertheless, it was a labor of love and worth every minute. I wouldn't have wanted it any other way.

After my beloved husband became ill, and after Judy decided to retire in early 2014, it was my time to retire in 2016. I had been in the PR field in South Florida for thirty-eight incredible years as well as numerous years before that in the Northeast. It had been a perfect journey, and I had had *an inside seat.*

PHOTOGRAPHY

The Adler Network's reception area displayed an entire wall of client press coverage. Maxine and Owen called it a "Wall of Fame."

Some Miss America Pageant contestants aboard a new Donzi Z-65 sportfisherman during the Atlantic City Boat Show ('80s).

Maxine and Owen at the White House in Washington,
DC, for a Very Special Arts event (1989).

Maxine with Jimmy Connors at a seniors' tennis tournament at the Boca
Raton Resort and Club. The event was sponsored by *Palm Beach Illustrated*
when Maxine served on that magazine's advisory board (early '90s).

Joan Weinberg of Macramates presented Audrey Hepburn with a large fiber mural representing children around the world during a UNICEF event at the Broward Center for the Performing Arts in Fort Lauderdale (1992).

A time capsule ready to be buried at the groundbreaking for Townsend Place. Boca Developers' partners with representatives of the city and the Boca Raton Resort and Club (1997).

Owen with mimes at a Boca Developers event celebrating the opening of the new sales pavilion for the Aragon, Townsend Place, and Mizner Grand (1997).

Developer Neil Fairman of the Plaza Group, his wife Lisa, and designer Tommy Hilfiger at an event at the Palms in Fort Lauderdale (1997).

A waiter, Judy, Maxine, and a costumed "guard" at a British-themed event at Townsend Place (1999).

Arnold Palmer during a press conference at Mizner Country Club in Delray Beach. Palmer's company designed the golf course (2000).

Peter Max with Willie Trump at an art exhibit at Williams Island in Aventura (2000).

Maxine and Judy with a stilt walker at the "Celebration of Art, Architecture, and Life" event on the future site of Acqualina in Sunny Isles Beach (2001).

Maxine, Owen, Senator Hillary Clinton, and the Trump Group's
Michael Goldstein at a fundraiser in Georgetown (2001).

Comedian Freddie Roman, Judy, Maxine, and Owen at an "I Have a Dream"
Foundation of Miami gala at the Signature Grand in Davie (2002).

Golf legend Lee Elder flanked by representatives of Pavarini Construction at the Pavarini Golf Classic benefiting the "I Have a Dream" Foundation of Miami (2003).

Performers Jon Secada and Nestor Torres at the "Celebrating Latin Culture/Boca" event at Robb & Stucky in Boca Raton (2003).

Owen, Judy, and Maxine with vintner Rob Mondavi at a wine-tasting event for One Bal Harbour condominium buyers at the Sea View Hotel in Bal Harbour (2003).

Celebrated Miami Chef Michelle Bernstein sampling her Latin bouillabaisse at a "Taste of the Future" event at the One Bal Harbor sales and model center in Bal Harbour (2003).

A "newsboy" actor and Judy during a cruise aboard a one-hundred-seventy-foot superyacht in Fort Lauderdale, to commemorate the launch of sales for the Waves Las Olas (2004). The loft project was never built.

The dramatic implosion of Harbour House North to make way for the new One Bal Harbour residential and hotel condominium (2004).

Maxine with former CNN Style editor Elsa Klensch at a Robb
& Stucky book signing in Boca Raton (2004).

Owen and Judy. *"From the time I joined the Adlers' agency in 1996, Owen treated
me with kindness and always looked out for me. He was like a big brother."*—Judy

Jules and Stephanie Trump with Joel and Alan Matus, pictured with "Dionysus," the Roman god of wine, at a broker event for the Luxuria condominium in Boca Raton (2005).

Maxine (right) with two *Palm Beach Post* colleagues at the grand opening of Verano in Port St. Lucie (2007).

Greg Norman addressed the press about his new signature golf course at Jupiter Country Club (2008).

Sabrina Kleier-Morgenstern, Michele Kleier, and Samantha Kleier-Forbes at the HGTV *Selling New York* filming event at One Thousand Ocean in Boca Raton (2011).

LXR Luxury Resorts' Jamie Telchin with sisters Venus and Serena Williams at an event marking the grand opening of the V-Starr Interiors furnished model at One Thousand Ocean (2012).

Venus Williams (right) with a mother and daughter being helped by the Lotus House shelter and resource center in Miami (2014).

PHOTO CREDITS

ACKNOWLEDGMENTS

FROM MAXINE: I WILL FOREVER be grateful to my family who continue to be a blessing to me, as they were to Owen. This book is a legacy reflecting the work that was important to both of us over the years. Their love and our work made "Grammy" and "Poppy" the individuals we both became. My love to my children, Jeffrey, Honey, and Robin; to my grandchildren, Jackie and Josh, Lauren and Justin, Jamie, Remy, and Zack; and to my great grandchildren, Jacob, Jordyn, Daniella, Jack, and one more bundle of joy on the way. And, of course, much appreciation to my beloved brother and sister-in-law, Bill and Lucie Schwartz.

From Judy: I thank Doug Black for learning very quickly that by supporting my work on this book, I would be a very happy writer *and* an even happier life partner. You own my heart. I am indebted to my daughters, Stephanie Goldstein Lavarias and Alison Goldstein, for encouraging me along my own life's journey, as well as the journey leading to this book. You are true gifts. And to my grandson Ben (who excels in science), reading and writing *are* also important! I also express gratitude to Eason Dobbs, Arline Horne, Sally Cameron, and Sherry Friedlander for kick-starting my career. In addition, I send appreciation to Ron Kumin, as well as to Al Padron, Carlos Leo, and Felipe Ponzoa, for putting their faith in me and allowing me to start PR divisions for their advertising agencies.

We send our appreciation to Lisa Gabrielson, an associate editor with Bonnier Corporation, who granted us permission to use writer John Clemans's words from his 1988 article about the Donzi Dash in *Motor Boating & Sailing*, which is no longer being published.

A sheynem dank (thank you very much) to Leah Rosenberg for helping us with the Yiddish terminology used in chapter 2 of this book.

The Adler Network would not have been successful without the diverse roster of clients whom we served over the years. We appreciate the confidence you placed in us.

Several vendors, in particular, never disappointed us and always made us look good: Silver Sac Catering (Karin); the Boca Raton Resort and Club's banquet department (George); Brantley Photography (Robert and Carmel); Andrew Goldstein Photography (Andrew); Florida Trade Graphics (Denny); K2 Graphics (Bruce); the La Mystique entertainment troupe (Rita and Len); Rafael and Juliana Productions (Rafael and Juliana); Designs By Sean (Sean and Alex); and Unity Productions (Serge).

Our heartfelt indebtedness to Venus Williams for the graciousness and generosity she provided to us and our clients off the tennis court. We also acknowledge the support of the ever-energetic "other" Adler—Elaine Adler of the Aventura Marketing Council. And we are forever grateful to Michele Kleier, Sabrina Kleier-Morgenstern, and Samantha Kleier-Forbes of Kleier Residential in New York City, former co-stars of HGTV's *Selling New York* and coauthors of *Hot Property*. All of you ladies rock!

We thank Lewis Goodkin of Goodkin Consulting for his "right on" real estate vision, opinions, and expert advice and for allowing us to quote him over the years.

Last but certainly not least, we appreciate the interest, respect, and response we received from members of the media. Many of you were more than our colleagues; you were our friends. We are particularly grateful to have had Gary Press, Linda Marx and Jana Soeldner Danger in our lives. Likewise, we were fortunate to have known Paige Rense; Olivia Hammar; Phyllis, Jeff, and Barbara Lichtenstein; Annette Galbo; Karen King; Susan Sherman; Gloria Blake; Esther Jackson; Susan Preville; Sheldon, Regina and Martin Birnbach; Sue Lynn; Bernie and Mark McCormick; Merri Grace McLeroy; Nila Do; Jennifer Tormo; Bernie Moran; Christiana Lilly; Jason Binn; Courtland Lantaff; Jordan Melnick; Eric Newell; Bill Kearney; Jared Shapiro; Michelle Simon; Robert and Madison Freeman; Dale King; Stephanie Murphy; Skip Sheffield; José Lambiet; John and Margaret Mary Shuff; Marie Speed; Kevin Kaminski; Brad Mee; Ronald Woods; Ila Fox Ardleigh; Daphne Nikolopoulos; Robin Hodes;

Allison Reckson; Sherman Robbins; Kim Mosley; Marina Brown; Susan Sherman; Ted Curtis; Nancy Christie; Deborah Hartz-Seely; Jennifer Pfaff; Steven Brown; Mary Gibble; Hortense Leon; Adam Goodkin; Maxine Hakimi; Jenny Bart; Linda Litsky Behmoiras; Felicia Levine; Linda Haase; Kay Renz; Lori Capullo; Roberta Klein; Sarah Harrelson; Hortense Leon; Helen Hill; Christine Davis; John Annuziata; Amy Keller; Richard Westland; Christina Woods; Pam Jaccarino; Glenn Hoffer; Steve DeWolf; Kevin Murphy; Deborah LaFogg Docherty; Garrett Foster; Ron Kukulski; Sheldon Greenberger; Willie Fernandez; David Hays; Charlyne Varkonyi-Schaub; Barbara Marshall; Mark Gauert; Cindy Kent; Cindy Metzger; Paul Owers; Jeff Zbar; Robyn Friedman; Brittany Wallman; Rod Stafford Hagwood; Dana Banker; Miriam Valverde; Johnny Diaz; Howard Saltz; Gretchen Day-Bryant; Doreen Christensen; Jody Rees; Lois Solomon; Meredith Clements; Michael Mayo; Howard Greenberg; Martha Gross; Jack Zink; Barbara Roop; Rick Menning; Tracy Kolody; David Bittner; Randy Brightman; Pam Doto; Kari Barnett; Marci Shatzman; Joanie Cox; Phyllis Steinberg; Dan White; Alan Goch; Michael Cumella; Jon O'Neill; Arnie Rosenberg; Ruben Cueto; Anne Vasquez; Susan Bryant; John Tanasychuk; Liz Balmaseda; Tom Peeling; Jake Kline; Chuck Strouse; Luis Rigual; Patrick Danner; Nora Bulnes; Lizbet Fenandez; Olivia Alvarez; Jenny Starr Perez; Larry Hirsch; Amit Bloom; José Alfonso Niño; Ugo Campello; Kevin Gale; Brian Bandell; Melanie Dickinson; Darcie Lunsford; Ed Duggan; Shaun Bevan; Mark Freerks; Leslie Kraft Burke; Eileen Cukler; Ashley Torres; Oscar Pedro Musibay; Robert Sims; Joan Fleischman; Rick Hirsch; Mindy Marques; Mindi Bernarde; Rose Novatny; Joan Chrissos; Jane Wooldridge; Martha Brannigan; Jorge Rojas; Harriet Johnson Brackey; Ida Cordle; Margarita Pardo Abrishami; Carla Canedo Cartier; Barbara DeLollis; Rick Christie; Alexandra Clough; Greg Stepanich; Larry Aydlette; Staci Sturrock; Antonio Fins; Bill DiPaolo; Carolyn DiPaolo; Pat Beall; Bill Husted; Jodie Wagner; Barbara Marshall; Katie Diets; Tanya Wade; Michelle Bernzweig; Perry Grant; Chris DeStefano; Mike Hetherington; Ava Van de Water; Craig Dolch; Jeff Ostrowski; Kimberly Miller; Susan Salisbury; Mary Thurwachter; Elliot Kleinberg; Mary Hladky; Emily Roach; Carol Rose; Bonnie Chynoweth; Tim Burke; Kevin Van Der Werff; Darrell Hofheinz; Aggie Ash; Joyce Reingold; Shannon Donnelly; Jay

Rees; Deborah Espana; Eric Kalis; David Lyons; George Haj; Catherine Wilson; Christy Heady; Ina Lee; Grace Delanoy; Carol Zalis; Janet Verdeguer; Sean Reid; Gail Gill; Michael Lewis; Michael Miller; Dennis Durkee; Mark Tomasik; Tammy Raits; Kit Bradshaw; Brightman Brock; Irwin Spivak; Darren Smith; Joyce Garret; Jeannette Stark; Dahlia Jean Weinstein; Lauren Brant Anscher; Cary Roman; Pat Curry; Mary Kate Leming; Amy Woods; Thom Smith; Jeffrey Cull; Scott Simmons; Betty Wells; Todd Shyrock; Olivia Wolff; Sergio Diment; Joshua Manning; Lynn Tiffany; Audrey Diamond; Suzanne Antonich; Glenn Fisher; Russell Spadaccini; Armando Portela; Deborah Ramirez; Pat Mascola; Tim Byrd; Alexander Brittell; Emily Schmall; Mark Maurer; Luis Perez; Ziata Faerman; Betty Cortina-Weiss; Allison Aronov; Flora Gerber; Anna Nezhurine; Rhenne Leon; Helen Hill; Bari Auerbach; Andrew Cotton; Mindi Rudan; Carol Boucard; Alejandro Aquirre; Joyce Brooks; Matt Siegel; Judith Faerron; John Clemans; Marilyn Mower; Rebecca Cahilly; Terry Purdam; Robert Pitts; Shannon Coates; Bob LaRue; Jim Martz; Linda Brockman; Scott Kauffman; Danielle Reed; Brooke Lange; Jens Kramer; Jennifer Gould Keil; Nancy Keates; June Fletcher; Christina Lewis; Charles Passy; Brett Anderson; Larry Bean; Bob Morris; Lori Bryan; Jeff Mann; Randy Shearin; Chris Thorn; Scott Judy; Linda Barr O'Flanagan; Kim Singletary; Nick Slevin; Sule Aygoren; Mamie Walling; Hugh Malone; Judith Tibbs; Cynthia Ayotte; Stephanie Mayhue; David Moran; Tim Ahern; Elizabeth Sherrod; Randall Forsyth; John Salustri; Kara Wetzel; Sara Polsky; Mary Lu Abbott; Shari Barbanel; Kathleen Carline-Russell; Lauren Varga; Ray Allegrezza; Karen Curran; Robin Jay; Robin S. White; Janet Allon; Susan Feinman; Iris Benaroia; Shari Kulha; Robert Leibman; Jill Keene; Dan Shube; David Weir; Pat Murphy; Corey Saban; Stephanie Sayfie; Meg Porter Berns; Odette Burton; David Gould; Steve Boyer; Robin Cross; Cathleen O'Toole; Terri Parker; Shayli Argota; Lynette Jennings; Cam Frierson; Meredith Lerner; Christine Fahey; and numerous others.

Some of the persons mentioned in *An Inside Seat*, as well as in this acknowledgments section, are no longer with us. We mourn their loss and remember them with fondness.

WORD PLAY FOR PR WRITER WANNABES

~~

Here are some words about the importance *and* perception of words in the public relations profession.

Words matter. They are extremely powerful. So choose them carefully. Especially in our technologically advanced world, with instant messaging, e-mails, tweeting, and other social media, it's easy for misperceptions to occur.

I had always preferred driving thirty miles to visit a client and talk face-to-face rather than to send off a fax or quick e-mail in which my facial expressions and tone of voice couldn't be seen or heard. But newer methods of communication have increasingly become the way of doing business and sharing relationships. So beware of what you put into writing. Once it's "out there," it is permanent. In addition, be certain to express yourself clearly and correctly because words are a direct reflection on you and your skills.

While Maxine was busy trying to right the many wrongs in this world, I was...writing.

I started out as an advertising copywriter, where my words were clever and catchy. I subsequently had to learn to write for the PR industry. It is a very different way of using words. You need to know, at minimum, how to construct a basic press (aka news) release for the media—one that won't end up in an editor's trash can. Or, in more modern times, be deleted from an e-mail. It is an inverted triangle with the answers to who, what, when, where, why, and how included in the first several sentences. That's because editors have limited space and may need to cut short what you have submitted to them, if they decide to use your news item.

Editors cut from the bottom up, so the pertinent facts should be as close to the top as possible.

Good grammar and correct spelling are required, of course, but you don't have to be an English major. Through the years, Maxine and I interviewed several English teachers, as well as attorneys, who wanted to change their careers and go into the public relations field. But their grammar was too strict and too formal. They oftentimes used big words that were not understandable to the average person when they could have selected an easier way to express themselves. Because they didn't want to modify their writing styles, they were not suited for the job.

Also, as a PR writer, you shouldn't get attached to your words. An editor has the right to change them for publication. For a few years, I was in love with the phrase "came to fruition," but it didn't fly as far or as often as I would have liked it to! So I stopped using it.

I've been fortunate throughout my career to have had most of my news releases and feature articles published verbatim. Having been a newspaper editor myself, I knew what other editors were looking for.

You have to become comfortable with the use of the AP (Associated Press) Stylebook, which is widely used as a writing and editing reference in newsrooms worldwide. It might as well be called the Bible, because it dictates the particular usage of words and the style of using words—where to place them, whether to capitalize them, and so forth. As an example, per this style guide, numbers from one to nine should be spelled out. Numbers ten and above should be numerals. If you affix a title to someone, it should either be written "Joe Schmo, vice president of XYZ Corporation," or "XYZ Corporation Vice President Joe Schmo." See what I mean?

AP style differs from the writing style found in the Chicago Manual of Style frequently used as a guide for the book publishing industry.

Back in the early eighties when I worked at another public relations firm, my employer hired a terrific newsman and a staunch journalist from one of Florida's daily newspapers. His writing was excellent but too straightforward and a bit dry for PR. I was told to "loosen him up." I taught Jack to use superlatives but warned that they must be attributed to someone saying them. A press release shouldn't read like a paid advertisement. Don't make the claim that something is "the best" (unless that "something" won an award giving it that distinction). You can, however, quote someone in a press release who gives their opinion that it is "the best." It took Jack a while, but after he relaxed and got the hang of things, he became a wonderful PR writer. Eventually, he became an adjunct professor in the mass communications department at Florida International University. When he called on me a few times to substitute for him, I felt honored.

When writing a feature article and not straight news, there is more leeway. You can be more creative. I've written hundreds upon hundreds of articles of this nature and had fun with them. That also has been the case for first-person essays (experiential articles) I've written and sold as a freelancer. You have greater word freedom and can even get cute by adding a pun or two or using a play on words. Just don't overdo it.

I was an early writer and have loved writing ever since. I began jotting my thoughts and feelings in the diary I received for my tenth birthday. Although I had a lot of friends growing up, sometimes I preferred being alone with my words. They were my playmates. I'm sure that's why I am a much better writer than a speaker!

I've written on typing and computer paper, torn scraps, stationery, and even on facial tissues that held my tears of inspiration. I've scribbled at school, at work, in cars and restaurants, on airplanes, and in my sleep where I dreamed the words to place upon the pad resting by my bedside.

Of course, I occasionally make typos and grammatical errors. I'm not perfect. But rereading my text again and again helps me detect those errors. If not, someone else will. The fewer corrections an editor has to make, the better the chance of the work being published.

Writing to meet a deadline is very different from having the luxury of time to wait until inspiration strikes. Most of my writing through the years was "on demand" and hurried. It didn't matter if I was inspired or not. I had to put the pedal to the metal. And I had to do it while multitasking and encountering interruptions (calls from clients, requests from the media, a crisis in the office, personal distractions, etc.). Now that I am retired and writing solely for myself (or, in this case, working with Maxine on this memoir), I am in an altered state. I am frantically trying to capture the words swirling around in my head. They are my only focus. I am lost and loving it. I know what I want readers to think, feel, and experience. When my words work, it's not work at all. It is rapture and a rush.

Writing as a craft, with all of the elements that go into it, must be studied. Still, even though you may possess the skill, you also have to have a whole lot of luck.

We wish you the *best*!

ABOUT THE AUTHORS

COLLECTIVELY, THE AUTHORS HAVE MORE than eighty years of experience in their field of expertise.

From her first public relations position in the health care industry in Passaic, New Jersey, at the start of seventies, until her retirement in 2016 from the South Florida PR agency she presided over for thirty-eight years, Maxine Adler enjoyed a career rich with experience and achievement.

As an icon, particularly of luxury design and real estate-focused PR, Adler had an inside seat while helping her clients successfully meet challenges and turn their visions and plans into reality.

Judy Goldstein began her career writing advertising copy in New York City and Miami before working as a writer/editor in the print media and PR fields in South Florida. A seasoned professional, she joined Adler's agency as vice president in 1996 and retired in 2014.

Goldstein's press releases and feature articles have been published locally, nationally, and internationally. Additionally, she authored a collection of free verse, *At Forty: Poems from the Heart.*

HOW TO ORDER THIS BOOK

THE PRINT PAPERBACK OF *An Inside Seat* can be ordered through the Amazon.com website. The e-book version may be ordered and downloaded from your Kindle device or through any electronic device that supports the Kindle application, including the iPad, iPhone, and so on.

www.ingramcontent.com/pod-product-compliance
Lightning Source LLC
Chambersburg PA
CBHW071417180526
45170CB00001B/136